HAIKUS INSPIRED BY TSUREZURE GUSA

PART 3

HAIKU COLLECTION XXVII
MAYUMI ITOH

In Memoriam,

Yoshida Kenkō

Contents

List of Photographs..vi

Notes on the Text..x

Acknowledgments...xiii

Introduction...1

Chapter 1..7

Chapter 2...27

Chapter 3...47

Chapter 4...67

Chapter 5...87

Chapter 6..107

Chapter 7..127

Chapter 8..147

Chapter 9..167

Chapter 10...187

Selected Bibliography...205

About the Author..211

List of Photographs

All paintings used in this book are in the public domain.
The recent photographs are credited below.

Photograph 0: "Portrait of Kenkō- hōshi" (Yoshida Kenkō),
Kikuchi Yōsai (1788–1878), uploaded by
Hannah~commonswiki, March 13, 2006, licensed by
Wikimedia Commons, https://commons.wikimedia.org/
wiki/File:Yoshida_Kenko.jpg.

Photograph 1: "Geisha and Copies of *Tsurezure-gusa*"
(with snipe flying over the river), c. 1766, Suzuki
Harunobu (c. 1725–1770), licensed by Wikimedia
Commons, https://upload.wikimedia.org/wikipedia/
commons/d/dd/Harunobu.The_Shoji_Screen.jpg.

Photograph 2: "*Tsurezure-gusa* Saga Edition" (showing Essay 173 about Ono no Komachi, on the left page), c. 1605-1624, uploaded by Underbar dk, December 25, 2017, licensed by Wikimedia Commons, https://commons.wikimedia.org/ wiki/File:Tsurezuregusa_Sagabon_ver._Toyo_Bunko.jpg.

Photograph 3: "Shinsen Temple Garden," Kyoto, Kyoto prefecture, January 2, 2011, taken by 663highland, licensed by Wikimedia Commons, https://commons.wikimedia.org/wiki/File:Shinsenen_Kyoto_Japan03n.jpg.

Photograph 4: "Painting of Cosmetics Box for Essay 191, *Tsurezure-gusa*," 1800–1850, Art Institute of Chicago, licensed by Picryl, https://picryl.com/media/passage-191-hyaku-kyujuichi-dan-from-the-series-essays-in-idleness-for-the-a88c3c.

Photograph 5: "Two Bamboo Trees at Seiryō Imperial Palace" (with *kure take* on the right and *kawa take* on the left), Kyoto, Kyoto prefecture, April 14, 2017, taken by Saigen Jiro, licensed by Wikimedia Commons, https://ja.wikipedia.org/wiki/清涼殿#/media/ファイル:Kyoto-gosho_Seiryoden_zenkei-2.jpg.

Photograph 6: "Kegon Falls," Nikkō, Tochigi prefecture, April 11, 2014, taken by Jordy Meow, licensed by Wikimedia Commons, https://ja.wikipedia.org/wiki/華厳滝#/media/ファイル:Kegon_Taki.jpg.

Photograph 7: "Sano Tsuneyo in the Story 'Potted Trees,'" 1890, Mizuno Toshikata (1866–1908), licensed by Wikimedia Commons, https://ja.wikipedia.org/wiki/佐野源左衛門#/media/ファイル: Kyodō_risshi_no_motoi,_Sano_Tsuneyo.jpg.

Photograph 8: "Shira-bōshi" (Court Dancer Lady Shizuka), c. 1825, Katsushika Hokusai (c. 1760–1849), licensed by Wikimedia Commons, https://ja.wikipedia.org/wiki/静御前#/media/ファイル:Shizuka-gozen_in_her_farewell_ dance_to_Yoshitsune.jpg.

Photograph 9: "Kitsune no yomeiri" (Fox Wedding), Katsushika Hokusai (c. 1760–1849), licensed by Wikimedia Commons,https://ja.wikipedia.org/wiki/狐の嫁入り#/media/ファイル:Hokusai_Kitsune-no-yomeiri.jpg.

Photograph 10: "Painting of White Plum Blossoms and Red Camelias for Essay 237, *Tsurezure-gusa*," 1800–1850, Art Institute of Chicago, licensed by Picryl, https://picryl.com/media/passage-237-nihyaku-sanjunana-dan-from-the-series-essays-in-idleness-for-the-203801.

Notes on the Text

This bilingual book presents each haiku in both Japanese
and English so that non-Japanese-speaking readers can
fully appreciate it. The first page for a given haiku (on the
left side) shows the original haiku in Japanese, which is
made up of a combination of Chinese characters (*kanji*) and
Japanese phonetic characters (*hiragana* and *katakana*). In
accordance with the customs for writing haiku, the old
spellings of *hiragana* are used for the original haiku.

Then, in order to facilitate a better understanding,
the original haiku is shown in a modern spelling in
hiragana and *katakana*. This allows readers to see how the
haiku is exactly pronounced phonetically. There are many
ways to pronounce specific *kanji* words, and the original
Japanese haiku does not indicate how each *kanji* word is
actually pronounced. It is sometimes difficult even for
Japanese readers to know the pronunciation. Therefore, the

simpler rendition of each haiku only in modern *hiragana*

and *katakana* will help. Afterward, the identification of the

season word—an essential element in haiku—for the haiku

is given and some explanations of the cultural and

historical backgrounds are added where applicable.

On the second page for a given haiku (on the right

side), a romanization of the original Japanese haiku is

provided, first, so that English-speaking readers can

understand how the haiku is pronounced. The words in

Roman letters are divided into smaller groups of syllables,

for easier reading.

Then, an English translation of the haiku is

presented. It is a paraphrasing of the haiku, rather than a

literal translation, in order for it to make the best sense in

English. Due to the structural differences in English and

Japanese, for many cases, the word order of the haiku

might be different from the original haiku in Japanese. It is followed by the English translations of the season word for the haiku and the explanations of the cultural and historical backgrounds. This completes the presentation of a given haiku.

All translations, including those of haikus, were made by the author. For romanizing Japanese words, the Hepburn style is primarily used, with macrons. However, macrons are not used for words known in English without macrons, as for Kyoto and Tokyo. Another exception is that "n" is not converted to "m" for words where it precedes "b, m, and p." Examples include tonbo (dragonfly), instead of tombo; sanma (saury), instead of samma; and tanpopo (dandelion), instead of tampopo.

Names of Japanese persons are given with the surname first, except for those who use the reversed order in English. Honorific prefixes, such as doctor and mister, are not used in the text, except in direct quotations.

Acknowledgments

This is the twenty-seventh haiku collection written by this author. I would like to thank all the members of *the Hoshi no shima kukai* (a new name for the Haiku Society of New York), Michael Bowers, Kent Calder, Toshiko Calder, Morrell Chance, Steve Clemons, Akiko Collcutt, Gerald Curtis, Linda Eckert, Martin Heijdra, Hoshi Hiroshi, Ronald Hrebenar, Imai Sanae, Itō Yayoi, Kumi Kato, Ellis Krauss, Sidney Lowe, Toshiyuki Nishikawa, Stephen Roddy, Hiroaki Sato, Shinji Sato, Tomoko Shibata, Anna Shields, Susan Stewart, Megumi Watanabe, Watanabe Miyuki, and Vicki Shigekuni Wong, for continuous encouragement and inspiration. I extend my appreciation to Meg Hamilton and Gregory Rewoldt for generous support.

The 670th anniversary of Kenkō-hōshi's death,

March 2022

Introduction

Photograph 0: "Portrait of Kenkō- hōshi" (Yoshida Kenkō), Kikuchi Yōsai (1788–1878), uploaded by Hannah~commonswiki, March 13, 2006, licensed by Wikimedia Commons, https://commons.wikimedia.org/wiki/File:Yoshida_Kenko.jpg.

Tsurezure-gusa (*lit.*, "idle essays") by 'Yoshida' Kenkō (1283–1352; generally known as "Kenkō-hōshi" [Monk Kenkō] and hereafter; his real surname was arguably Urabe; Yoshida was possibly the name the family assumed in the 15th century). The 243 essays written by this hermit-like monk in Kyoto in the mid-14th century are characterized by witty anecdotes and wise aphorisms, as well as by deep insight into arts and aesthetics.

Tsurezure-gusa is in fact considered one of The Three Great Essays in Japanese classic literature, along with *Makura no sōshi* ("the pillow book") by the court lady Sei shōnagon (c. 966–c. 1025) and *Hōjō-ki* ("journal of a ten-foot-square hut") by the poet/monk Kamo no Chōmei (1155–1216). The importance of *Tsurezure-gusa* was such that it was adopted in Japanese classic literature classes in public high schools throughout Japan.

Kenkō-hōshi was from a reputable Shinto family that served as officials at the Department of Shinto Affairs of the Imperial Court. His father, Urabe Kaneaki, was a priest at Yoshida Shrine in Kyoto and served Emperor Go-Uda and other emperors. Kenkō-hōshi became a butler for Horikawa Tomomori (1249–1316), the Minister of the Center and Imperial Palace Guard General. The Horikawa family was a branch family of the Koga family, the main line of the Murakami-Genji clan, descended from Emperor Murakami (924–967). Tomomori's daughter Horikawa Motoko (Kishi, 1269–1355) was a consort of Emperor Go-Uda and birthmother of Emperor Go-Nijō (1285–1308).

Being well versed in classic literature, Kenkō-hōshi was a renowned calligrapher and poet so much so that he was referred to as one of the Four Great Poets of that time. Around the age of 30, however, Kenkō-hōshi resigned from his position at the Imperial Court and became a monk (the real reason for his resignation is not established). He then devoted himself to practicing Buddhism teaching and writing poetry in Kyoto, Osaka, and elsewhere.

Specifically, Kenkō-hōshi lived on the premises of Enryaku Temple in Yokawa at the foot of Mt. Hiei (northeast of Kyoto, in current Ōtsu, Shiga prefecture). He also lived on the premises of Shugaku-in Temple in the hills in northeastern Kyoto (the Shugaku-in Imperial Palace Villa was built on this location in the mid-17th century). He sometimes lived in Shōen Temple in Abeno, Osaka, where two stone monuments of Kenkō-hōshi were erected. Later in his life, he moved to Narabi-ga-oka, near Omuro Nin'na Temple, in the northwest of Kyoto, where he wrote *Tsurezure-gusa*.

It is also known that Kenkō-hōshi traveled twice to Kamakura (in current Kanagawa prefecture), the seat of the Kamakura shogunate government. He lived in Jōgyō Temple in Mutsuura (in current Kanazawa, Yokohama). There, he befriended Hojō Kanesawa (not Kanazawa) Sadaaki (1278–1333), the 12th Assistant Regent and 15th Regent (briefly) of the Kamakura shogunate. Sadaaki

restored and expanded the Kanesawa Bunko (library),
created by his grandfather, Hojō Kanesawa Sanetoki
(1224–1276). This was the first comprehensive, organized
library made by a samurai and housed a wide collection of
important archival documents. It still exists today as the
Kanazawa Bunko.

*   *   *

This haiku collection (2022) is a homage to *Tsurezure-gusa*
and presents original haikus written by this author, inspired
by Kenkō-hōshi's essays. Part III refers to Essay 163
through Essay 243 by Kenkō-hōshi (a total of 81 essays)
and introduces 89 original haikus by this author, with
annotations where applicable.

It is not the purpose of this anthology to translate
whole essays in *Tsurezure-gusa* into English; however, a
summary of some essays is given in the annotations, where
applicable. For English translations of the essays, see
Yoshida Kenkō, *Essays in Idleness: The Tsurezuregusa of
Kenkō*, translated by Donald Keene (1967, 1998, 2006).

Chapter 1

Photograph 1: "Geisha and Copies of *Tsurezure-gusa*" (with snipe flying over the river), c. 1766, Suzuki Harunobu (c. 1725–1770), licensed by Wikimedia Commons, https://upload.wikimedia.org/wikipedia/ commons/d/dd/Harunobu.The_Shoji_Screen.jpg.

第百六十三段

長月や

　　太衝の点

　　　有りや無しやと

ながつきや

　　たいしょうのてん

　　　ありやなしやと

季語　長月（ながつき、旧暦の九月、晩秋）

太衝（たいしょう）は、陰陽道で、九月の異称。「太」の漢字
は、「太」か「大」について、論争する御所の陰陽道者の段。

Essay 163.

Naga tsuki ya

    Taishō no ten

        ariya nashiya to

September

    The word Taishō has a dot or not

      That is the question

Season word: Naga tsuki (*lit.*, "long month," September in the old calendar; late autumn)

Kenkō-hōshi refers to the debate of Onmyōdō (divination) officials at the Imperial Court on whether the word Taishō ('September' for Onmyōdō) is spelled with a dot or not.

第百六十四段

歌雲雀

　　　ピーチクパーチク

　　　　朝日和

うたひばり

　　　ピーチクパーチク

　　　　あさびより

季語　雲雀（ひばり、三春）
「おしゃべりは、概して、他愛のないものが多く、無益である」と説く兼好法師。「沈黙は金なり」という諺もある。この句は、熊本県の民謡、「おてもやん」（「若い女中さん」のこと）に拠る。

Essay 164.

Uta hibari

    piichiku pāchiku

        asa biyori

The lark

    is singing loudly

        in the fine morning

Season word: uta hibari (singing lark; all spring)

Kenkō-hōshi says that chatting is mostly meaningless and

useless. This haiku refers to a traditional local folksong in

Kumamoto prefecture about a young female maid.

第百六十五段

雪深し

　　　金剛峯寺の

　　　　　　修行僧

ゆきふかし

　　　こんごうぶじの

　　　　　　しゅぎょうそう

季語　　雪（ゆき、晩冬）
「顕教・密教に限らず、僧が本山を離れて俗世の人と交わることは見苦しい」と言う兼好法師。弘法大師空海（774年–835年）の確立した真言密教は、護摩行などの修業を重んずる。816年、高野山（こうやさん）に金剛峯寺を創建。

Essay 165.

Yuki fukashi

    Kōngōbu ji no

        shugyō sō

Deep snow

    the monk is practicing

        at Kōngōbu Temple

Season word: yuki (snow; late winter)

Kenkō-hōshi thinks that it is disgraceful for monks, either of esoteric or open Buddhism, to socialize with secular people. Kūkai (774–835), the founder of the esoteric Shingon Buddhism, built Kōngōbu Temple on Mt. Kōya.

第百六十六段

雪仏

　　過疎の村里

　　　　消える時

ゆきぼとけ

　　かそのむらざと

　　　　きえるとき

季語　雪仏（ゆきぼとけ、雪達磨、ゆきだるま、晩冬）
「人の営みは、春に雪仏を作って、それを安置するための
お堂を建てるが、お堂が完成する前に雪仏は溶けてしまう
というように、儚いものである」と説く兼行法師。

Essay 166.

Yuki botoke

 kaso no mura zato

  kieru toki

The snowman

 the deserted mountain village

  is disappearing

Season word: yuki botoke (*lit.*, "snow buddha," snowman;

late winter)

Kenkō-hōshi considers that man's life is futile like building

a shelter for a snow buddha in spring; the snow buddha

melts before the completion of the hut.

第百六十七段　1

昼行灯

　　一休さんの

　　　　夜ながかな

ひるあんどん

　　いっきゅうさんの

　　　　よながかな

季語　　夜なが（よなが、三秋）
「自己の優越さを奢ってはならず忘れるべきである」と説く
兼好法師。「大智は愚の如し」、「大賢は愚なるが如し」と
いう言葉がある。臨済宗大徳寺派の僧、一休宗純（そうじ
ゅん、1394 年–1481 年）は、風狂（奇行）で知られるが、詩
人で、能書家であった。「一休さんの頓知話」で知られる。

Essay 167-1.

Hiru andon

　　Ikkyū san no

　　　　yonaga kana

The daytime lamp

　　Monk Ikkyū is studying

　　　　late into the night

Season word: yonaga (long night in autumn; all autumn)

Kenkō-hōshi says that a man should not show off the
superiority in his expertise, but should forget it. Ikkyū
Sōjun (1394–1481) was known for his peculiar behavior
and witty riddles, but was a respectable monk at Daitoku
Temple in Kyoto, and a refined poet.

第百六十七段　2

行燈の

　　蝋燭痩せる

　　　　雪の夜

あんどんの

　　ろうそくやせる

　　　　ゆきのよる

季語　雪（ゆき、晩冬）

学べば学ぶ程、自己の無知を知る。学ぶことの奥深さ、際
限のなさを痛感する日々であるが、「この年齢になって、知
らないことがあったとは驚いた」と言った人がいたことに、
驚いた。

Essay 167-2.

Andon no

    rōsoku yaseru

        yuki no yoru

The candle of the lamp

    is getting short

        in the night of snow

Season word: yuki (snow; late winter)

The saying that the more one studies the more one finds his
ignorance seems to hold true, but a person once stated, "I
was surprised to find at this stage of life that there was
something I did not know." This was astonishing.

第百六十八段

木菟や

　　　賢者の聲の

　　　　　響く森

みみずくや

　　　けんじゃのこえの

　　　　　ひびくもり

季語　木菟（みみずく、耳のような羽角のある梟、三冬）
「老いて、一つの専門分野に秀でていても、やはり、謙虚
でいることが望ましい」と考える兼好法師。この句は、西洋
では、梟が賢者の象徴と見做されていることに因む。

Essay 168.

Mimizuku ya

    kenja no koe no

        hibiku mori

The horned owl

    the voice of the wiseman

        reverberates in the woods

Season word: mimizuku (horned owl; all winter)

Kenkō-hōshi considers that even if a senior man was
perfected in one expertise, he should remain humble and
not show it off. This haiku refers to the Western culture in
which owls are considered a symbol of wisdom.

第百六十九段

春の波

　　　建礼門院の

　　　　　嘆き

はるのなみ

　　　けんれいもんいんの

　　　　　なげき

季語　　春の波（はるのなみ、三春）
「〜の式という用法は、建礼門院平徳子（1155 年-1214 年、平
清盛の娘）に仕えた右京大夫（うきょうのだいぶ）が再度宮中に
出仕した時に既に使っていた」と説く段。有職故実（ゆうそくこじ
つ、朝廷や武家の行事、法令、儀式、制度、官職の先例）に詳
しい兼好法師。徳子は壇ノ浦の戦（1185 年 4 月）で入水した息
子安徳天皇（1178 年-1185 年）の後を追うが、助命された。

Essay 169.

Haru no nami

    Kenreimon in no

        nageki

Spring sea waves

    the grief

        of Empress Tokushi

Season word: haru no nami (sea waves in spring; all spring)

Kenkō-hōshi says that the word 'ceremony' in the way it is used now was already used by Ukyō-no-dayū, the lady-in-waiting for Empress Tokushi (1155–1214). This haiku refers to Tokushi, whose son Emperor Antoku (1178–1185), threw himself into the sea after defeat in the Battle of Dan-no-ura in April 1185.

第百七十段

秋海棠

　　親しき友と

　　　　静かに会話

しゅうかいどう

　　したしきともと

　　　　しずかにかいわ

季語　秋海棠（しゅうかいどう、初秋）

「他人の家に行って長居をするのは良くないことである。一方、特に用事もないのに人が訪ねて来て、静かに一時（いっとき）を過ごすことは、実に良いことである」と言う兼好法師。

Essay 170.

Shūkaidō

    shitashiki tomo to

        shizukani kaiwa

The hardy begonia

    the quiet conversation

        with the bosom friend

Season word: shūkaidō (hardy begonia; early autumn)

Kenkō-hōshi says that it is impolite to visit someone's house and stay for a long time talking. In turn, he finds it pleasant when a close friend visits you unannounced and spends a quiet time together for a while.

Chapter 2

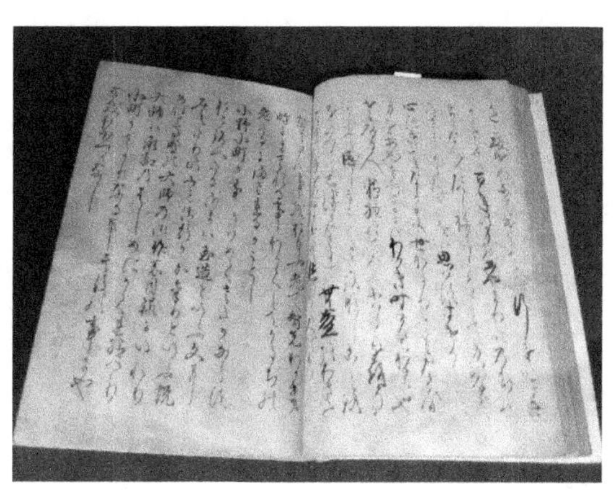

Photograph 2: *"Tsurezure-gusa* Saga Edition" (showing Essay 173 about Ono no Komachi, on the left page), c. 1605-1624, uploaded by Underbar dk, December 25, 2017, licensed by Wikimedia Commons, https://commons. wikimedia.org/ wiki/File:Tsurezuregusa_Sagabon_ver. _Toyo_Bunko.jpg.

第百七十一段

貝合

　　　二見ヶ浦の

　　　　　夫婦岩

かいあわせ

　　ふたみがうらの

　　　　めおといわ

季語　　貝合（かいあわせ、雛祭りの遊び、仲春）
「貝覆ひ（貝合）のような遊びから治世に至るまで、万事、事に
当たるには、外を見るのではなく、手許をよく見極めて行うべき
である。そうすればそれが波及して外にも良い効果をもたらす」
と説く兼行法師。二枚貝は、他の貝とはぴったりと合わせられな
いことから、末長い夫婦の象徴とされた。この句は、西行や芭蕉
に倣い、貝の二身（身と殻）と二見ヶ浦にかける。

Essay 171.

Kai awase

    Futami g aura no

        Meoto iwa

The clam matching game

    and the Couple Rock

        at Futami Cove

Season word: kai awase (clam matching game, to match
the two shells of a clam; mid-spring)
Kenkō-hōshi says that in doing things, ranging from the clam
matching game to governing the nation, one should deal with the
immediate issues right in front of you, first, rather than remote
issues. Clam shells only match in their own pair (with the other
half); hence they are regarded as a symbol of a long marriage.
This haiku refers to a pun of clam matching and the Couple Rock
in Iso, Mie prefecture, per Saigyō and Bashō.

第百七十二段

薄墨桜

　　百の遷宮

　　　　見守りて

うすずみざくら

　　ひゃくのせんぐう

　　　　みまもりて

季語　薄墨桜（うすずみざくら、晩春）
「若い時は、血気盛んで過ちを起しがちであるが、年を取ると心が動じなくなり、無益なことをしなくなる」と言う兼行法師。この句は、岐阜県根尾谷にある樹齢 1500 年以上の江戸彼岸（エドヒガン）の古木、薄墨桜を詠む。伊勢神宮は、20 年毎に内宮と外宮にある神殿の遷宮をする。

Essay 172.

Usuzumi zakura

    hyaku no sengū

        mimamori te

The Usuzumi cherry blossoms

    have seen the transfer of Ise Grand Shrine

        one hundred times

Season word: Usuzumi zakura (Usuzumi cherry blossoms; late spring)

Kenkō-hōshi says that when a man gets older his mind becomes stable and he stops doing futile things. This haiku refers to the 1,500-year-old cherry tree in Gifu prefecture and to the every 20-year transfer of the inner and outer shrines at Ise Grand Shrine in Mie prefecture.

第百七十三段

苧環や

　　　小野小町の

　　　　　衣の色

おだまきや

　　　おののこまちの

　　　　　きぬのいろ

季語　苧環の花（おだまきのはな、晩春）
六歌仙、三十六歌仙の中で唯一の女性、小野小町を考
証する段。恋多き、絶世の美女として知られるが、生没年
は不詳。「花の色は　移りにけりな　いたづらに　我が身世
にふる　ながめせし間に」（『古今集』）で有名。苧環の花に
は、紫、青、紅、ピンク、黄、白などの様々な色がある。

Essay 173.

Odamaki ya

Ono no Komachi no

kinu no iro

The columbine

the color of the silk kimono

of Ono no Komachi

Season word: odamaki (columbine; late spring)

Kenkō-hōshi writes about Ono no Komachi, who was the
only female poet among the Six Great Ancient Poets and
the Thirty-six Great Ancient Poets. She was also known as
a great beauty, but her birthyear and year of death are
unknown except that she lived in the nineth century.

第百七十四段

鷹狩や

　　猟犬駆ける

　　　　嵯峨の丘

たかがりや

　　りょうけんかける

　　　　さがのおか

季語　　鷹狩（たかがり、三冬）
「小鷹狩（小型の鷹を使って鶉、雲雀などの小鳥を捕える）
用の犬を大鷹狩（鶴、雁、兎などを捕える）に使うと、小鷹
狩には適さなくなる」という例を挙げて、「大事な道（仏道）
に精進すれば、小事を忘れることができる」と説く段。

Essay 174.

Taka gari ya

    ryōken kakeru

        Saga no oka

The falconry

    the hunting dog is running

        around the hills of Saga

Season word: taka gari (falconry; all winter)
Once a hunting dog for small-prey falconry was used for
large-prey falconry, it is no longer suitable for the former.
Likewise, Kenkō-hōshi says that once a man finds a big
goal (to serve in Buddhism), he will abandon small
(secular) matters.

第百七十五段　1

山桜

　　酒呑童子の

　　　　　大暴れ

やまざくら

　　しゅてんどうじの

　　　　　おおあばれ

季語　山桜（やまざくら、晩春）

人に酒を無理やり勧めて飲ませることの非を説く兼好法師。
この句の酒呑童子は、丹波国（現、京都府辺り）の大江山
に住んでいた伝説上の鬼の頭目。御伽草子や謡曲などの
題材となる。

Essay 175-1.

Yama zakura

    Shuten dōji no

        ō abare

The mountain cherry blossoms

    the Drunkard Demon

        is rampaging

Season word: yama zakura (mountain cherry blossoms;
late spring)
Kenkō-hōshi is against forcing people to drink. This haiku
refers to the wicked demon in a folktale, who lived on Mt.
Ōe in Tanba (current Kyoto prefecture) and did mischief in
the capital.

第百七十五段　2

酔芙蓉

　　午後の一杯

　　　　ほどほどに

すいふよう

　　ごごのいっぱい

　　　　ほどほどに

季語　酔芙蓉（すいふよう、初秋）

強いる酒の席を厳しく非難する一方、「節度を保ちながら、友人と酒を酌み交わすことは、楽しいものだ」と言う兼好法師。酔芙蓉の名前は、午前中は、花は白いが、午後になるとピンクに変わることに由来。

Essay 175-2.

Sui fuyō

gogo no ippai

hodo hodo ni

The cotton rosemallow

Restrain the afternoon drinking

to a reasonable amount

Season word: sui fuyō (cotton rosemallow, *hibiscus mutabilis cv. versicolor*; early autumn)
While opposing forcing people to drink, Kenkō-hōshi finds it enjoyable to drink sake with friends occasionally. This haiku refers to cotton rosemallow, which changes its color from white in the morning to pink in the afternoon.

左近の桜

　　　紅きお顔の

　　　　　左大臣

さこんのさくら

　　　あかきおかおの

　　　　　さだいじん

季語　　左近の桜（さこんのさくら、雛段の飾り、仲春）
この句は、雛祭の雛壇に飾る「左近の桜」（向かって右側）と、その隣に座る左大臣（白髯を付けた赤ら顔の年配の武将）を詠む。童謡「うれしいひなまつり」の「赤いお顔の右大臣」は、「左大臣」（右大臣より上の位）の誤り。右大臣（若い武将）は、向かって左側、「右近の橘」の隣に座る。

Essay 175-3.

Sakon no sakura

   akaki o kao no

      Sadaijin

The Cherry Blossoms of the Left

   and the red face

      of the Minister of the Left

Season word: Sakon no sakura (Cherry Blossoms of the

Left for the Hina Doll Festival, March 3; mid-spring)

This haiku refers to the Cherry Blossoms of the Left and

the Minister of the Left in a hina doll set, a miniature

reproduction of the Shishin Imperial Palace.

第百七十六段

若菜摘む

　　小松の帝

　　　　白き御手

わかなつむ

　　こまつのみかど

　　　　しろきみて

季語　若菜摘む（わかなつむ、新年）
「黒戸の御所」（くろど、京都御所清涼殿の北側の廊にあった細
長い部屋）は、小松御門（帝）光孝天皇（830年–887年、在位、
884年–887年）が、自炊をしていた不遇時代を忘れないよう、
薪の煤で黒くなった部屋をそのまましておいたことに由来すると
言う段。この句は、小松帝の「君がため　春の野に　出でて　若
菜摘む　わが衣手に　雪はふりつつ」（「百人一首」）を引用。

Essay 176.

Wakana tsumu

Komatsu no mikado

shiroki mite

Picking the seven plants

Emperor Komatsu

his hands are white

Season word: wakana tsumu (picking the 'seven plants' on
January 7; new year)

Kenkō-hōshi tells that the Black-Door Room in Seiryō Imperial
Palace derives from Emperor Kōkō (Komatsu, 830–887), who
left it black (from soot) as a reminder of his unfortunate years
when he cooked for himself. This haiku quotes his poem.

第百七十七段

梶の鞠

　　　大鋸屑を敷く

　　　　　鎌倉の御所

かじのまり

　　　おがくずをしく

　　　　　かまくらのごしょ

季語　梶の鞠（かじのまり、梶鞠、かじまり、初秋）

鎌倉幕府第 6 代将軍宗尊親王（むねたか、1242 年–1274 年）の御鞠（蹴鞠、けまり、しゅうきく）の会で、雨に濡れた庭を乾かすため、重臣佐々木政義が、おがくずを献上して敷いたので人々は感心した。これを聞いた京都の吉田中納言は、「おがくずは賎しい物である。砂の用意をしておくことが昔からの作法」であると一蹴したという話。この句の梶鞠は、蹴鞠の家元、京都飛鳥井家の邸宅跡の白峯神社で、七夕の日に行われる蹴鞠会のこと。鞠を梶の木の枝に掛けて、七夕二星（牽牛星、織女星）に手向けたことに因む。

Essay 177.

Kaji no mari

    ogakuzu o shiku

        Kamakura no gosho

The kemari game on July 7

    the sawdust is being scattered

        on the garden of Kamakura Palace

Season word: kaji no mari (the kemari game on July 7;
early autumn)

When Kamakura government sixth shogun Prince Munetaka
(1242–1274) held a kemari game (ancient football), the garden
was wet from rain. His aide Sasaki Masayoshi brought sawdust
and scattered in on the garden. People were impressed with this
quick fix, but an Imperial Court official in Kyoto said, "Sawdust
is lowly. Sand should have been ready per old custom." This
haiku refers to the kemari game on July 7.

Chapter 3

Photograph 3: "Shinsen Temple Garden," Kyoto, Kyoto prefecture, January 2, 2011, taken by 663highland, licensed by Wikimedia Commons, https://commons.wikimedia. org/wiki/File:Shinsenen_Kyoto_Japan03n.jpg.

第百七十八段

御神楽や

　　　草薙の剣

　　　　　いづこなり

みかぐらや

　　　くさなぎのつるぎ

　　　　　いづこなり

季語　　御神楽（みかぐら、旧暦の十二月中旬、仲冬）

「宮中の御神楽を見た侍たちが、天皇が草薙の剣（三種の神器の一つ）を持っていたと言ったのに対し、清涼殿から別殿に行幸される際は、夜御殿に安置されている宝剣ではなく、昼御座（ひのござ）にある剣を持っていくと、女房が正した」という段。御神楽は、宮中で神座に神を迎え、歌舞を奉納する神道の神事。草薙の剣は、平家滅亡時、安徳天皇の入水と伴に失われた。以後、代りの宝剣が、熱田神宮（愛知県名古屋市）に祀られる。

Essay 178.

Mikagura ya

    Kusanagi no tsurugi

        izuko nari

The Shinto Dance

    at the Imperial Court

        Where is the Sacred Sword of Kusanagi?

Season word: mi kagura (Shinto Dance ceremony at the
Imperial Court; mid-winter)

When a Shinto Dance ceremony was held at the Imperial Court,
warriors said that they saw the emperor carrying the Sacred
Sword of Kusanaki. Hearing this, a lady-in-waiting stated, "That
is not the Sacred Sword of Kusanagi. The emperor carries a
substitute sword when he leaves Seiryō Imperial Palace." This
haiku refers to the Sacred Sword of Kusanagi that was lost in the
sea in 1185 with Emperor Antoku (1178–1185). A substitute
sword is enshrined in Atsuta Shrine in Nagoya, Aichi prefecture.

第百七十九段

平等院

　　北の大門

　　　　西の蓮池

びょうどういん

　　きたのだいもん

　　　　にしのはすいけ

季語　　蓮池（はすいけ、晩夏）

宇治平等院の建立に際し、地形上、大門を北にせざるを得な
かったことについて関白藤原頼通（992 年–1074 年）から、その
是非を問われた大学頭（だいがくのかみ）中納言大江**匡房（お
おえのまさふさ、1041 年–1111 年）**が、「インドの那蘭陀寺（なら
んだじ）大門は北向きである」と答えて安心させたという段。その
根拠は不明であるが、唐の西明寺の大門は北向きである。

Essay 179.

Byōdō in

    kita no dai mon

        nishi no hasu ike

Byōdō-in Temple

    the Main Gate to the north

        and the lotus pond to the west

Season word: hasu ike (lotus pond; late summer)
The chief advisor to the emperor, Fujiwara no Yorimichi (992–
1074), was concerned that the main gate of Byōdō-in Temple
had to be built north of the temple (facing north) against the
custom that the main gate was built to the south (facing south)
and asked the scholar Ōe no Masafusa (1041–1111). He
answered, "No problem. The main gate of Naranda Temple in
India faces north." There is no literature to prove this, but the
main gate of Saimyō (Ximing) Temple in China faces north.

第百八十段　1

左義長や

　　どんどん燃やせ

　　　毬の杖

さぎちょうや

　　どんどんもやせ

　　　まりのつえ

季語　　左義長（さぎちょう、旧暦の小正月に行う、新年）

左義長（三毬杖）を説明する段。宮中で正月に行う打毬
（ホッケーのような球技）に使った毬杖（ぎちょう、毬を打つ
ための杖）を、小正月（旧暦1月15日）に、大内裏の真言
院（密教の修法に場所）から−に移して焼き上げる宮中行
儀のこと。民間の「どんど焼き」の起源となる。

Essay 180-1.

Sagichō ya

 Don don moyase

  mari no tsue

The stick burning ceremony

 Burn, burn

  hockey sticks

Season word: Sagichō (stick burning ceremony, January 15; new year)

Kenkō-hōshi explains that the stick burning ceremony is conducted on January 15 in the old calendar to transfer the sticks of a dakyū game (ancient hocky) played at the Imperial Court on New Year's Day to the Imperial Shinsen (Shinzen) Temple Garden and burn them.

第百八十段　2

神泉苑

　　空海の知る

　　　　花の宴

しんせんえん

　　くうかいのしる

　　　　はなのえん

季語　　花の宴（はなのえん、桜の花見の宴、晩春）

平安京最古の史跡、神泉苑は、平安京大内裏に接して造園された禁苑（天皇のための庭園）で、歴代天皇の宴遊地となる。812 年には、嵯峨天皇が初めて桜の「花宴の節（せち）」を催したことにより、「花見の発祥地」と言われる。824 年の旱魃の際、弘法大師空海（774 年-835 年）が、祈雨（雨乞いの儀式）を行って以来、雨乞いの霊池となる。

Essay 180-2.

Shinsen en

Kūkai no shiru

hana no en

Shinsen Garden

Kūkai might have seen

that cherry blossom viewing party

Season word: hana no en (cherry blossom viewing party;
late spring)
Imperial Shinsen Temple Garden was known for the origin of
cherry blossom viewing as Emperor Saga held it for the first
time in 812. Until then, 'flower viewing' referred to plum
blossom viewing per Chinese tradition. During a drought in 824,
Shingon Buddhism founder Kūkai (774–835) prayed
successfully for rain at the lake of the garden.

第百八十一段

粉雪や

　　　　丹波の里の

　　　　　　白き臼

こなゆきや

　　　　たんばのさとの

　　　　　　しろきうす

季語　粉雪（こなゆき、晩冬）

「粉雪」の語源は、米をついてふるいにかける時に出る白

い粉に似ていることに由来するという段。

Essay 181.

Kona yuki ya

Tanba no sato no

shiroki usu

The powder snow

the white grinder

of the village in Tanba

Season word: kona yuki (powder snow; late winter)

Kenkō-hōshi explains that the white powder that falls on a

grinder while sifting rice is the origin of the word 'powder

snow.'

第百八十二段

乾鮭や

　　隆親卿の

　　　　面目躍如

からざけや

　　たかちかきょうの

　　　　めんぼくやくじょ

季語　　乾鮭（からざけ、干鮭、三冬）
乾鮭は、鮭の腸（はらわた）をとって乾（しらぼし）にしたもの。料
理の名人大納言四条隆親卿（しじょうたかちか、1202 年−1
279 年）が、天皇に乾鮭を供したことに難癖をつけた人に対して、
「乾鮎を供することには問題がない。ならば、乾鮭を供すること
に何の問題があろうか」と機知に富んだ返答をしたという段。

Essay 182.

Kara zake ya

    Takachika kyō no

        menboku yakujo

The dried salmon

    Lord Takachika

        his face was saved

Season word: kara zake (dried salmon; all winter)

This is an episode of Lord Shijō Takachika (1202–1279), who was a gourmet cook. When he served a dried salmon to the emperor, someone said, "Is there any rule to serve such a lowly thing?" He responded by saying, "Is there any rule not to serve a dried sweetfish? There isn't. Then, there is no problem to serve a dried salmon."

第百八十三段

牛の角突

　　　山古志村の

　　　　　ヘリコプター

うしのつのつき

　　　やまこしむらの

　　　　　ヘリコプター

季語　牛の角突（うしのつのつき、うしずもう、初夏）
「人を突く牛や人を嚙む馬の角や耳を切り、印とすることは、法律
で定められた飼い主の義務である」という段。新潟県山古志村（現、
長岡市）の牛の角突（牛角力）は、国指定重要無形文化財の伝統
行事。2004年、新潟県中越地震で被災し、70頭いた闘牛の半数
が犠牲となった。生き残った飼養牛、約110頭を1頭ずつ、ヘリコ
プターで救出した。牛の角突の復活には10年かかった。

Essay 183.

Ushi no tsuno tsuki

    Yamakoshi mura no

        herikoputā

The bull sumo

    the rescue helicopter

        in Yamakoshi village

Season word: ushi no tsuno tsuki (bull sumo; early summer)

Kenkō-hōshi says, "Horns of bulls that attack people are cut and ears of horses that bite people are cut. It is a crime of the owner of animals not to put such markers on animals that harm people. This haiku refers to the traditional bull sumo in Yamakoshi village (current Nagaoka, Niigata prefecture). The area was hit by a major earthquake in 2004 and rescue operations saved the surviving bulls, one by one, by helicopter.

第百八十四段

障子張る

　　　執権の母

　　　　　白き月

しょうじはる

　　　しっけんのはは

　　　　　しろきつき

季語　　月（つき、三秋）

鎌倉幕府第5代執権北条時頼（1227年-1263年）の母松下禅尼
が時頼に質素倹約を教える段。時頼の訪問前に、破れた障子を
張り替えている禅尼を見て、兄の安達義景（1210年-1253年）が、
「誰かに全部一度に張り替えさせましょう」と言うと、禅尼は、「物は
修理して使うものだということを時頼に教えるために、こうしているの
です」と答えたという。鎌倉武士は質素倹約で知られた。

Essay 184.

Shōji haru

   shikken no haha

     shiroki tsuki

Fixing the paper-screen door

   the Regent's mother

     under the white moon

Season word: tsuki (moon; all autumn)

This episode refers to Nun Matsushita, the mother of the fifth
regent of the Kamakura shogunate, Hōjō Tokiyori (1227–1263).
At his homecoming, his mother was fixing paper-screen doors.
Her brother Adachi Yoshikage (1210–1253) said, "You do not
have to fix them. Have someone change the entire doors." She
said, "I am doing this to teach my son to be frugal." Kenkō-
hōshi writes, "Frugality is the essence of governing the nation."

第百八十五段

流鏑馬や

　　　生き馬の

　　　　　目を抜く弓矢

やぶさめや

　　　いきうまの

　　　　　めをぬくゆみや

前段の安達義景（1210 年-1253 年）の三男、陸奥守（むつのか
み）安達泰盛（1231 年-1285 年）が、馬乗りの名手であったとい
う逸話。この句は、流鏑馬（端午の節句に行われた神事）を詠
む。「生き馬の目を抜く」は、素早く物事をする様を表す。

Essay 185.

Yabusame ya

iki uma no

me o nuku yumi ya

The mounted archery

the arrow is running

as fast as the horse

Season word: yabusame (Shinto mounted archery
ceremony; mid-summer)
This episode introduces Adachi Yoshikage's third son, the
governor of Mutsu (the whole northeastern region of Japan),
Adachi Yasumori (1231–1285), who was a fine horse rider. This
haiku refers to the Shinto mounted archery ceremony conducted
on May 5 in the old calendar.

Chapter 4

Photograph 4: "Painting of Cosmetics Box for Tsurezure-gusa Essay 191," 1800–1850, Art Institute of Chicago, licensed by Picryl, https://picryl.com/media/passage-191-hyaku-kyujuichi-dan-from-the-series-essays-in-idleness-for-the-a88c3c.

第百八十六段

八幡宮

　　駿馬の憩ふ

　　　春の岡

はちまんぐう

　　しゅんめのいこう

　　　はるのおか

季語　春（はる、三春）

「吉田という馬乗りが、馬は力ずくで扱うのではなく、その馬の長
短を知ることが肝要である」と言った段。この句は、鎌倉幕府を
開いた源頼朝（1147 年−1199 年）の祖先、源頼義（988 年
−1075 年）が、1063 年、京都の石清水八幡宮を勧請した鶴岡
若宮を起源とする鶴岡八幡（現神奈川県家鎌倉市）に集められ
た馬を詠む。

Essay 186.

Hachimangū

   shunme no ikou

      haru no oka

Hachiman Shrine

   the fine horse is resting

      on the hill in spring

Season word: haru (spring; all spring)

Kenkō-hōshi writes, "A horse rider by the name of Yoshida said that you should not deal with a horse by force. You should know the character of each horse before riding." This haiku refers to horses brought to Tsuruoka Hachiman Shrine in Kamakura, Kanagawa prefecture, which was founded in 1063 by Minamoto no Yoriyoshi (988–1075), the ancestor of Minamoto no Yoritomo (1147–1199), the founder of the Kamakura shogunate.

第百八十七段

炎帝や

　　　歩み続ける

　　　　　　亀の道

えんていや

　　　あゆみつづける

　　　　　　かめのみち

季語　炎帝（えんてい、三夏）

「道を極める秘訣は、たゆまず慎重に努力することである。

上手くても好き放題にするのは失敗の元である」と説く兼

好法師。この句は、イソップ寓話の「兎と亀」より連想。

Essay 187.

Entei ya

　　ayumi tsuzukeru

　　　kame no michi

The scorching sun

　　the tortoise keeps walking

　　　on the road

Season word: entei (scorching sun; all summer)

Kenkō-hōshi says, "The secret of perfecting one's expertise

is to keep making an effort." This resonates with "The

Tortoise and the Hare" in Aesop's Fables.

第百八十八段　1

鵜の匠

　　　長良の川の

　　　　　夜の白む

うのたくみ

　　　ながらのかわの

　　　　　よのしらむ

季語　鵜の匠（うのたくみ、鵜匠、うじょう、三夏）
「物事を極めるには脇道にそれず、その一事に専心すべきである」と説く兼好法師。この句は、岐阜県岐阜市の長良川鵜飼を詠む。鵜飼で獲る鮎は古来より珍重され、鵜匠は、時の権力者により保護されてきた。現在も、宮内庁式部職鵜匠という職名が与えられ、補助金が支給される。

Essay 188-1.

U no takumi

     Nagara no kawa no

          yo no shiramu

The cormorant trainer

     the night on the Nagara River

          is getting light

Season word: u no takumi (ujō, ushō, cormorant trainer for

fishing for sweetfish; all summer)

Kenkō-hōshi says, "To perfect one expertise, one should

not be sidetracked, but focus." This haiku refers to the

traditional cormorant fishing on the Nagara River in Gifu,

Gifu prefecture.

第百八十八段　2

藤の花

　　僥倖を呼ぶ

　　　　藤井四段

ふじのはな

　　ほうぎょうをよぶ

　　　　ふじいよんだん

季語　　藤の花（ふじのはな、晩春）

兼好法師は囲碁の達人。この句は、14 歳 2 ヶ月で四段に昇段
するなど、多くの最年少記録を保持する将棋棋士藤井聡太九
段（2002 年生まれ）を詠む。礼儀正しく謙虚な人柄で、2017 年
6 月 2 日の第 43 期棋王選予選決勝戦の勝利に際して（20 連
勝）、「連勝できたのは僥倖としか言いようがかい」と述べた。

Essay 188-2.

Fuji no hana

    hōgyō o yobu

        Fujii yondan

The wisteria blossoms

    Fujii of the Fourth Rank

        brings forth serendipity

Season word: fuji no hana (wisteria blossoms; late spring)

Kenkō-hōshi was good at playing 'go' (a boardgame). This haiku refers to Fujii Sōta (b. 2002), the youngest Japanese professional chess player (current ninth rank). Being humble by nature, he stated when he won the match 20 times consecutively, "This was nothing but serendipity."

第百八十九段

葉牡丹や

　　　人生の計

　　　　　量りかね

はぼたんや

　　　じんせいのけい

　　　　　はかりかね

季語　葉牡丹（はぼたん、晩冬）

「どれだけ周到な計画を立てても、人生は思い通りにはい

かない」と言う兼好法師。この句は、正月の飾りに欠かせ

ない葉牡丹を詠む。

Essay 189.

Habotan ya

jinsei no kei

hakari kane

The ornamental kale

it is hard to draw up

the new year's resolution

Season word: habotan (*lit.*, 'leaf peony,' ornamental kale;

late winter)

Kenkō-hōshi writes that life does not go as planned no

matter how meticulously you planned. This haiku refers to

ornamental kale, a must plant for the new year season, with

its bright purple and white leaves.

第百九十段

母子草

　　　風の便りに

　　　　　父を乞ふ

はこぐさ

　　　かぜのたよりに

　　　　　ちちをこう

季語　　母子草（ははこぐさ、晩春）

兼好法師は、女も子供も嫌いで、妻帯者になってはならな

いと説く。どんな女でも朝晩連れ寄り添っていると、気に食

わなくなり、憎たらしくなるので、通い婚が良いと勧める。

Essay 190.

Hahako gusa

    kaze no tayori ni

        chichi o kou

The mother and child plant

    begs the wind

        to bring the father

Season word: hahako gusa (*lit.*, 'mother-child plant,' jersey cudweed; late spring)

Kenkō-hōshi does not like women and children and is opposed to marriage. He says, "You will get tired of a woman if you live together for a long time and will end up hating her."

第百九十一段　1

夕化粧

　　揺れる香りの

　　　　奥ゆかし

ゆうげしょう

　　ゆれるかおりの

　　　　おくゆかし

季語　夕化粧（ゆうげしょう、白粉花、オシロイバナ、仲秋）
「昼間ではなく、夜に身だしなみを整えることこそ、真に奥ゆかし
いことである」と言う兼好法師。この句の夕化粧は、夕方に開き
翌朝に萎む一日花。紅、ピンク、白、黄、オレンジ、しぼり模様
などの花には芳香がある。黒い種の中の白い粉（胚乳）が化粧
の白粉（おしろい）のように見えることから白粉花と呼ばれる。

Essay 191-1.

Yūgeshō

    yureru kaori no

        oku yukashi

The four o'clock flower

    its drifting scent

        is deeply aesthetic

Season word: yūgeshō (four o'clock flower; mid-autumn)

Kenkō-hōshi writes that it is truly aesthetic to see a person minding and fixing up his/her appearance in the evening, rather than in the daytime. This haiku refers to yūgeshō (*lit.*, 'makeup in the evening'), whose fragrant flower blooms in the evening. The white powder contained in its black seedpods looks like makeup powder.

第百九十一段　2

夕顔や

　　　鏡に絡む

　　　　　長き髪

ゆうがおや

　　　かがみにからむ

　　　　　ながきかみ

季語　　夕顔（ゆうがお、晩夏）

夕顔（ユウガオ）は、ウリ科の蔓性の一年草。夕暮れに白い花を開き、翌朝には萎む一日花。干瓢（ひょうたん）に似た大きな実をつける。この句は、『源氏物語』第4帖「夕顔」を詠む。

Essay 191-2.

Yūgao ya

    kagami ni karamu

        nagaki kami

The white-flowered gourd

    her long hair

        entangles the mirror

Season word: yūgao (white-flowered gourd, bottle gourd;

late summer)

Yūgao (*lit.*, 'evening face') blooms in the evening and dies

the next morning. This haiku refers to the namesake lady

in "Yūgao," Chapter Four of *The Tale of Genji*, who dies

suddenly at dawn.

第百九十二段

百度石

　　　白鳧と

　　　　　急ぎ足

ひゃくどいし

　　　しろふくろうと

　　　　　いそぎあし

季語　　白鳧（白ふくろう、三冬）

「神社の参拝も、人気のない夜に行うのが良い」とする兼

行法師。この句の「百度石」は、御百度参りをする時の目

印として設けられた石のこと。

Essay 192.

Hyakudo ishi

shiro fukurō to

isogi ashi

The one-hundred-prayer stone

the snowy owl listens

to the hurried steps

Season word: shiro fukurō (snowy owl; all winter)

Kenkō-hōshi says that it is more aesthetic to visit shrines at
night when there are few people. This haiku is about the
one-hundred-prayer stone, which is placed at shrines as a
marker for those who go forth and back between the
entrance of the shrine and its main hall one hundred times
to pray for their wish to come true.

Chapter 5

Photograph 5: "Two Bamboo Trees at Seiryō Imperial Palace" (with *kure take* on the right and *kawa take* on the left), Kyoto, Kyoto prefecture, April 14, 2017, taken by Saigen Jiro, licensed by Wikimedia Commons, https://ja.wikipedia.org/wiki/清涼殿#/media/ファイル:Kyoto-gosho_Seiryoden_zenkei-2.jpg.

第百九十三段

空梅雨や

　　　西寺の僧の

　　　　　空威張り

からつゆや

　　　さいじのそうの

　　　　　からいばり

季語　　空梅雨（からつゆ、仲夏）
「自己の門外である事柄に口を挟むことは避けるべきである」と
言う兼行法師。この句は、824年の旱魃の際、淳和（じゅんなん）
天皇が、神泉苑で、東寺（とうじ）の空海（真言宗開祖弘法大師、
774年-835年）と西寺（さいじ）の守敏僧都（しゅびんそうず）に
祈雨（雨乞いの儀式）を競わせたエピソードを詠む。結果、空海
が勝ち、神泉苑は雨乞いの霊池となる。

Essay 193.

Kara tsuyu ya

    Saiji no sō no

        kara ibari

The dry spell in the rainy season

    the monk at Sai Temple

        is acting arrogant

Season word: kara tsuyu (a dry spell in the rainy season, mid-summer)

Kenkō-hōshi tells one should not meddle with something that is outside your expertise. This haiku is about the rain-begging prayer competition in 824, in which the founder of Shingon Buddhism, Saint Kūkai (774–835) at Tō Temple, won over Monk Shubin at Sai Temple.

第百九十四段　1

天満宮

　　「替えましょ、替えましょ」

　　　鷽替へる

　てんまんぐう

　　「かえましょ、かえましょ」

　　　うそかえる

季語　鷽替（うそかえ、1 月 7 日−1 月 25 日、新年）
嘘の虚構について考察する段。この句は、各地の菅原道真
（845 年−903 年）を祭神とする神社（天満宮）で行われる鷽替と
いう神事を詠む。去年の厄災を「嘘」にして開運招福を祈願する。
鳥の鷽（ウソ）にかけて、去年の木彫りの鷽を新しいものと交換
する。この句では、鷽（三春）は季語として使われていない。

Essay 194-1.

Tenman gū

   "Kaemasho, kaemasho"

     uso kaeru

Tenman Shrine

   "Let's exchange, let's exchange"

     The wood sculpture of a bullfinch

Season word: uso kae (*lit.* 'exchange a wood sculpture of a
bullfinch [lie]'; new year)
Kenkō-hōshi ponders lies, deceptions, and gullibility. This
haiku refers to a new-year rite at Tenman shrines to
exchange the last year's wood sculpture of a bullfinch (*uso*,
a pun on lie) with a new one, in order to make the bad
things that happened last year into lies and to pray for good
fortune in the new year.

第百九十四段　2

鶯替や

　　大統領の

　　　　ツイッター

うそかえや

　　だいとうりょうの

　　　　ツイッター

季語　鶯替(うそかえ、1 月 7 日−1 月 25 日、新年)

この句は、米議会襲撃事件など、トランプ元米大統領のツ

イッターによる暴動の煽動を示唆する。

Essay 194-2.

Uso kae ya

    Daitōryō no

        Tsuittā

To exchange the wood sculpture of a bullfinch

    to eliminate

        the President's Tweets

Season word: uso kae (*lit.* 'exchange wood sculpture of a

bullfinch [lie]'; new year)

This haiku alludes to the instigations of former president

Donald Trump, including that of the attack on Capital Hill.

第百九十五段

川涼し

　　　木彫りの地蔵

　　　　　洗ふ殿

かわすずし

　　　きぼりのじぞう

　　　　　あらうとの

季語　涼し（すずし、三夏）

立派で気品のあった久我通基内大臣（こがみちもと、源通基、1240 年-1309 年）が、奇行に走るようになった逸話について語る兼好法師。兼好法師が在俗中仕えていた堀川家は、村上源氏久我家の分流である。

Essay 195.

Kawa suzushi

    kibori no jizō

        arau tono

The cool river

    the lord is washing

        the wood statue of Little Buddha

Season word: suzushi (pleasant coolness in summer; all summer)

Kenkō-hōshi tells of an episode about Minister of the Right Koga Michimoto (1240–1309). He was a respectable and refined nobleman, but began to act strange. The Horikawa family that Kenkō-hōshi served was a branch family of Koga.

96

第百九十六段

東大寺

　　先払ひの儀

　　　　鹿の啼く

とうだいじ

　　さきばらいのぎ

　　　　しかのなく

季語　鹿啼く（しかなく、雄が雌を求めて鳴く声、三秋）
前段の久我通基内大臣（こがみちもと、1240 年–1309 年）が、右近
衛大将の時、東大寺の鎮守社、手向山（たむけやま）八幡宮の御
神輿が、東寺の鎮守社、若宮八幡宮から戻る際、先払い（貴人が
通るために通行人に道を空けさせること）をしたことを問われたが、
これは慣習に則った正しい処置であるときっぱりと答えたという段。

Essay 196.

Tōdai ji

   saki barai no gi

      shika no naku

Tōdai Temple

   the rite of clearing people off the road

      the deer cries out

Season word: shika no naku (deer cries out; all autumn)

Kenkō-hōshi tells of an earlier episode of Koga Michimoto (1240–1309) as General of the Right of the Imperial Palace Guard. When he escorted the return of the sacred body of the gods to the shrine at Tōdai Temple from a branch shrine, he cleared people off the road for the passing of the sacred palanquin. When he was questioned about this handling, he said he did so according to custom.

第百九十七段

雛壇の

　　三人官女

　　　澄まし顔

ひなだんの

　　さんにんかんじょ

　　　すましがお

季語　　雛段（ひなだん、雛祭の雛段、仲春）
「定額」（じょうがく）について考証する段。定額は、各寺に定員を定めて僧を置いたことを指し、その僧のことを「定額僧」と呼んだ。しかし、兼好法師は、「定額は、寺の僧だけでなく、官女を含め、定員が決まっている宮中の下級役人に共通して使われた呼称である」と述べる。この句は、雛祭の雛壇に飾る三人官女を詠む。

Essay 197.

Hina dan no

    san'nin kanjo

        sumashi gao

The Hina doll display steps

    the three court ladies-in-waiting

        look prim

Season word: hina dan (Hina doll display steps; mid-spring)

Regarding the word 'jōgaku' (quota), Kenkō-hōshi says that it not only refers to monks at temples but also to servants at the Imperial Court. This haiku refers to the three ladies-in-waiting hina dolls for the Hina Doll Festival on March 3.

第百九十八段

蓬摘む

　　籠の重たし

　　　　揚名介

よもぎつむ

　　かごのおもたし

　　　　ようめいのすけ

季語　蓬（よもぎ、三春）
「揚名」という役職名について詮議する段。揚名は、名目だけで、職務も俸給もない官職のことで、「揚名介」（ようめいのすけ、国司の次官のこと）に使われるのみならず、「揚名目」（ようめいのさかん、国司の四等官のこと）にも使われると説明する兼好法師。揚名介は、『源氏物語』第4帖「夕顔」に言及される。

Essay 198.

Yomogi tsumu

    kago no omotashi

        Yōmei no suke

Picking mugwort

    the basket of the fourth-rank clerk

        is heavy

Season word: yomogi (Japanese mugwort; all spring)

Kenkō-hōshi writes that the word 'yōmei" (a nominal rank
in the government that had neither an official job
description nor a salary) was not only used for deputy
governors of provincial states but also for the fourth-rank
clerk of the provincial governor.

第百九十九段

律の風

　　祇園精舎の

　　　　釈迦の夢

りちのかぜ

　　ぎおんしょうじゃの

　　　　しゃかのゆめ

季語　律の風（りちのかぜ、秋らしい趣きの風、三秋）
律音（りつおん）と呂音（りょおん）という雅楽の音階について考
証する段。横川（よかわ、比叡山三塔の一つ）の行宣（ぎょうせ
ん）法印によると、「中国は呂音の国で、律音はない。一方、日
本は律音のみの国で、呂音はない」という段。この句は、琵琶法
師の語る『平家物語』を引用。

Essay 199.

Richi no kaze

   Gion shōja no

      shaka no yume

The graceful autumn wind

   Buddha is meditating

      at Jetavana Temple

Season word: richi no kaze (a graceful autumn wind like

an ancient musical scale; all autumn)

Regarding the ancient musical scales, 'ritsu' and 'ryo,'

Kenkō-hōshi writes, "Grand Monk Gyōsen at Yokawa, part

of Mt. Hiei Enryaku Temple, states that China uses only the

'ryo' scale, whereas Japan uses only the 'ritsu' scale." This

haiku quotes *The Tale of the Heike*, which was recited by

biwa (lute-like string instrument) monks.

第二百段

若竹や

　　　内親王の

　　　　　遊ぶ庭

わかたけや

　　　ないしんのうの

　　　　　あそぶにわ

季語　若竹（わかたけ、仲夏）

清涼殿（天皇の日常の居所であった内裏の殿舎）の庭に
植えられた二本の竹について講釈する兼好法師。呉竹（く
れたけ、向かって右側）は葉が細く、河竹（かはたけ、漢竹、
向かって左側）は葉が広いと説明する。

Essay 200.

Waka take ya

    naishin nō no

        asobu niwa

The young bamboo

    the princess is playing

        in the imperial garden

Season word: waka take (young bamboo; mid-summer)

Kenkō-hōshi assesses two species of bamboos—kure take

(with broader leaves) and kawa take (with slenderer

leaves)—planted in the garden of the Seiryō Imperial

Palace, the residential palace of the emperor.

Chapter 6

Photograph 6: "Kegon Falls," Nikkō, Tochigi prefecture, April 11, 2014, taken by Jordy Meow, licensed by Wikimedia Commons, https://ja.wikipedia.org/wiki/華厳滝#/media/ファイル:Kegon_Taki.jpg.

第二百一段

霊鷲山

　　釈迦の説法

　　　　鷲の聴く

りょうがせん

　　しゃかのせっぽう

　　　　わしのきく

季語　鷲（わし、三冬）

お釈迦様が霊鷲山（りょうじゅせん、インドのビハール州に
ある山）で説法した際、マガダ国のビンビサーラ王（紀元前
558年頃–紀元前491年頃）が霊鷲山に建てたという二つ
の卒塔婆について説明する段。

Essay 201.

Ryōga sen

   Shaka no seppō

      washi no kiku

Vulture Peak

   the eagle is listening

      to Buddha's preaching

Season word: washi (eagle; all winter)

Kenkō-hōshi explains the two stupas that the king of
ancient Indian Magadha, Bimbisāra (c. 558 BC–c. 491 BC)
is said to have built on Vulture Peak, where Buddha had
given a sermon.

第二百二段

神無月

　　出雲大社の

　　　　神々よ

かんなづき

　　いずもたいしゃの

　　　　かみがみよ

季語　　神無月（かんなづき、旧暦十月の異名、初冬）

神無月の語源について疑問を投げかける兼好法師。一般
には、十月に全国の神々が出雲大社に集まるので、各地
の神社では神が不在になることに由来すると言われる。

Essay 202.

Kan'na zuki

    Izumo taisha no

       kamigami yo

October

    the gods are gathering

       at Izumo Grand Shrine

Season word: Kan'na zuki (October in the old calendar; early winter)

Kenkō-hōshi questions the etymology of Kan'na zuki (*lit.*, "the month in which there are no gods"). It is generally believed that the gods gather at Izumo Grand Shrine in October in the old calendar so that there are no gods in all the other shrines in Japan in that month.

第二百三段

靫掲げ

　　　五條の宮へ

　　　　　厄詣

ゆぎかかげ

　　ごじょうのみやへ

　　　　やくもうで

季語　厄詣（やくもうで、厄払、やくばらい、晩冬）
厄除けに靫（ゆぎ、矢を入れる箱）をかける慣習を考証する段。
元々は、勅命により謹慎処分を受けた者の家に靫をかけた。五
條天神（元、「天使の宮」）は、天皇の御病気や疫病流行時に靫
をかけたことから、厄除・病気退散の神として信仰される。厄詣
は、節分の夜、厄年の人が神社に参詣して厄を落とすこと。

Essay 203.

Yugi kakage

    Gōjō no miya e

        yaku barai

Carrying the arrow box

    driving out the evil spirits

        at Gōjō Shrine

Season word: yaku mōde (ceremony to drive out the evil

spirits at a shrine; late winter)

Kenkō-hōshi examines the custom of driving the evil spirits

out by hoisting arrow boxes at Gōjō Shrine in Kyoto during

the sickness of emperors and during epidemics. Today this

ritual is conducted on the eve of the arrival of spring,

February 4.

第二百四段

七竈

　　拷問受くる

　　　　五右衛門の釜

ななかまど

　　ごうもんうくる

　　　　ごえもんのかま

季語　七竈（ななかまど、晩秋）
「鞭打の刑の作法があるが、その器具についても、その方法に
ついても、今は、わきまえる人はいなくなった」と言う兼好法師。
この句は、釜煎（かまいり）の刑に処せられた石川五右衛門
（1558 年頃−1594 年）を詠む。七竈は燃えにくい木で、七度竈
に入れても燃え残ることからの命名。紅葉と赤い実が際立つ。

Essay 204.

Nana kamado

   gōmon ukuru

      Goemon no kama

The burning rowan tree

   Goemon is being tortured

      in the boiling bathtub

Season word: nana kamado (Japanese rowan tree; late autumn)

Kenkō-hōshi deplores that the decorum for flagellation of criminals was forgotten. This haiku refers to Ishikawa Goemon (c. 1558–1594), a Robbin Hood-like thief in Kyoto, who was boiled alive as a punishment.

第二百五段

大瑠璃や

　　お大師様の

　　　　霊を呼ぶ

おおるりや

　　おだいしさまの

　　　　れいをよぶ

季語　　大瑠璃（おおるり、ヒタキ科の小鳥。三夏）
「比叡山延暦寺で、天台宗開祖、伝教大師最澄（767 年
―822 年）の御霊を勧請して起請文（きしょうもん、誓約書）を書
き始めたのは、慈恵（じえ）僧正（良源、延暦寺中興の祖、
912 年―985 年）である」と講釈する兼好法師。この句は、お大
師様、伝教大師最澄を詠む。オオルリは、姿が美しいのみなら
ず、声の美しさから、ウグイス、コマドリとともに三鳴鳥とされる。

Essay 205.

Ōruri ya

   o daishi sama no

      rei o yobu

The blue-and-white flycatcher

   is calling for the soul

      of Grand Monk Saichō

Season word: ōruri (blue-and-white flycatcher, a pretty songbird; all summer)

This is an episode about Grand Monk Jie (912–985), who rehabilitated Mt. Hiei Enryaku Temple by transferring a divided soul of Grand Monk Saichō (767–822), the founder of Tendai Buddhism. This haiku refers to Grand Monk Saichō.

第二百六段

あかのまま

　　　喰みし大牛

　　　　　そのままに

あかのまま

　　　はみしおおうし

　　　　　そのままに

季語　あかのまま（蓼の花、たでのはな、イヌタデ、初秋）
徳大寺公孝（藤原きんたか、1253 年−1305 年）が検非違使庁長官
の時、下級役人の牛が牛車から外れて庁舎の中に入り、横たわっ
てしまった。皆が牛を陰陽道師の所に送り御祓をすべきであると言
う中、公孝の父、太政大臣徳大寺実基（1201 年−1273 年）は、「そ
の必要なし。牛に分別はない」と言って牛をそのまま持ち主に返し
た。その後、不吉なことは何も起こらなかったと言う話。

Essay 206.

Aka no mama

    hamishi ō ushi

       sono mama ni

The knotgrass

    Let's leave the giant ox that ate it

       as it is

Season word: aka no mama (knotgrass; early autumn)

Kenkō-hōshi tells of an episode in which an ox of a lower-rank officer got loose and lay down inside the Police and Prosecutor's Agency, ruminating. Everyone felt that that was a bad omen and that the ox should be taken to a diviner, but Chancellor Tokudaiji Sanemoto (1201–1273) said, "There is no need to do so; the ox had no bad intentions." Nothing evil happened afterwards.

第二百七段

山棟蛇

　　嵯峨の亀山

　　　悔ひは無し

やまがかし

　　さがのかめやま

　　　くいはなし

季語　山棟蛇（やまがかし、蛇、へび、三夏）
前段の太政大臣徳大寺実基が、怪奇や迷信を恐れず合理的な判
断をした逸話。後嵯峨院が、嵯峨に亀山殿（仙洞御所、現.霊亀山
天龍寺）造営のため地ならしをした時に蛇が密集する塚がでた。
皆が、「この地の土神なので掘り捨ててはならない」と恐れたのに
対し、実基は、「鬼神は邪ではない。掘り捨てるべきである」と進言
した。塚を崩し、蛇を大井川に流したが、祟りはなかった。

Essay 207.

Yama gakashi

Saga no Kameyama

kui wa hashi

The tiger keelback snake

Kameyama Palace in Saga

has no regrets

Season word: yama gakashi (tiger keelback, a species of venomous snake; all summer)

Kenkō-hōshi tells of another episode of Chancellor Tokudaiji Sanemoto, who was not afraid of superstitions and made rational decisions. When Kameyama Palace for Retired Emperor Go-Saga was being built, a snake pit was found. Everyone felt that snakes were the land gods and should not be dug out. The chancellor said, "There is no need to be afraid and the snake pit should be dug out and disposed of." It was thrown into the Ōi River but nothing evil occurred afterwards.

第二百八段

華厳滝

　　真一文字の

　　　　紐のごと

けごんだき

　　まいちもんじの

　　　　ひものごと

季語　　滝（たき、三夏）
「華厳院（仁和寺の別院）の弘舜（こうしゅん）僧正が、経文
の紐の結び方について、『今、流行りの結び方は誤りであ
り、見苦しい』と言って、紐を解かせて、正しい結び方を教
えたという段。この句は、栃木県日光市にある華厳滝（けご
んのたき）を詠む。

Essay 208.

Kegon daki

   maichi monji no

      himo no goto

Kegon Waterfalls

   they flow down

      as if they were a straight string

Season word: taki (waterfall; all summer)

This is an episode of Monk Kōshun at Kegon Temple (a
subordinate temple of Nin'na Temple), who said, "The
popular way to tie Buddhist sutras is wrong and unsightly,"
and showed the correct way to do so. This haiku refers to
the Kegon Waterfalls in Nikkō, Tochigi prefecture.

第二百九段

他人の田の

　　稲を刈る人

　　　　捨案山子

ひとのたの

　　いねをかるひと

　　　　すてかがし

季語　稲刈（いねかり、晩秋）（稲刈が済んで用無しとなり捨てられた案山子、晩秋）
田の所有権の訴訟に負けて悔しがる人から、「その田の稲を刈ってこい」と言われ、その途中の田の稲も刈ってしまった使役人の理屈（元より、訴訟に負けた田の稲を刈る権利はないのだから、ついでに他の田の稲も刈った）を面白がる兼好法師。「盗みを一つするならば、二つしても同じである」というような理屈。

Essay 209.

Hito no ta no

    ine o karu hito

        sute gakashi

A servant is harvesting

    the rice of someone else's paddies

        where the abandoned scarecrow lies

Season words: ine kari (harvesting rice; late autumn) and sute gakashi (abandoned scarecrow left on the rice paddies; late autumn)

Kenkō-hōshi tells of an episode in which a servant harvested the rice of someone else's paddies on the way to harvest the rice of the paddies of his master, who had lost a lawsuit over the property. The servant's logic was that to harvest the rice of the land that his master had lost his rights to would be the same thing as to harvest the rice of someone else's land on the way.

Chapter 7

Photograph 7: "Sano Tsuneyo in the Story 'Potted Trees,'" 1890, Mizuno Toshikata (1866–1908), licensed by Wikimedia Commons, https://ja.wikipedia.org/wiki/佐野源左衛門#/media/ファイル: Kyodō_risshi_no_motoi,_Sano_Tsuneyo.jpg.

第二百十段

呼子鳥

　　　大和の里の

　　　　　吾子呼ばむ

よぶこどり

　　　やまとのさとの

　　　　　あこよばん

季語　　呼子鳥（よぶこどり、晩春）
『万葉集』、『古今和歌集』に謳われ、「古今伝授三鳥」と言われ
るも、正体不明な春鳥、「喚子鳥」について考証する段。鵺（ヌ
エ、虎鶫、トラツグミ、夏鳥）、鶯（ウグイス、春鳥）、時鳥（ホトトギ
ス、「郭公」とも書く、夏鳥）など諸説ある。この句は、高市黒人
（たけちのくろひと）の詠んだ、「大和には　鳴きて来らむ　呼子
鳥　象（さき）の中山　呼びそ超ゆなる」（『万葉集』）を引く。

Essay 210.

Yobuko dori

    Yamato no sato no

        ako yoban

The spring songbird

    Will you call for my child

        who lives in the village in Yamato

Season word: yobuko dori (spring songbird; late spring)

Kenkō-hōshi assesses the unidentified spring songbird called "yobuko dori," which was mentioned in famous ancient poem collections. It could refer to the Japanese bush warbler, lesser cuckoo, or scaly thrush, but this is not established. This haiku is after an ancient poem that mentioned the bird.

第二百十一段

寒椿

　　罪人赦す

　　　　寛永寺

かんつばき

　　ざいにんゆるす

　　　　かんえいじ

季語　寒椿（かんつばき、晩冬）

「万事において他人を頼りにしてはならない。頼れば裏切られ失望する。最初から物事に期待しなければ、失望せず傷つかずにすむ」と説く兼好法師。寛容、寛恕の精神の大切さ。この句に引用の寛永寺は、江戸幕府三代将軍、徳川家光（1604 年－1651 年）が、徳川将軍家の菩提寺として、1625 年、開基。

Essay 211.

Kan tsubaki

    zainin yurusu

        Kan'ei ji

The winter camellia

    Kan'ei Temple

        pardons the criminal

Season word: kan tsubami (winter camellia; late winter)

Kenkō-hōshi says that one should not rely on others, so you do not have to feel betrayed or disappointed and you can be tolerant of others' behavior. This haiku refers to Kan'ei Temple that the third Tokugawa shogun Iemitsu (1604–1651) founded as a family temple in 1625.

第二百十二段

名月や

　　　地球を想ふ

　　　　　かぐや姫

めいげつや

　　　ちきゅうをおもう

　　　　　かぐやひめ

季語　名月（めいげつ、仲秋）

秋の月を愛でる兼行法師。秋は空気が澄むので、月も、

はっきり見える。この句は、『竹取物語』の主人公、かぐや

姫を詠む。

Essay 212.

Meigetsu ya

    chikyū o omou

        Kaguya hime

The fine moon

    the Shining Princess is thinking

        of the people on earth

Season word: mei getsu (the fine moon of mid-autumn; mid-autumn)

Kenkō-hōshi admires the moon in autumn when the air is clear and crisp. This haiku refers to the story, *Taketori monogatari* (The Tale of the Bamboo Cutter), in which an old man finds a tiny girl in a bamboo and raises her as his daughter, but she returns to the moon in the end.

第二百十三段

炭火取る

　　手と狩衣の

　　　　いと白し

すみびとる

　　てとかりぎぬの

　　　　いとしろし

季語　　炭火（すみび、三冬）
「天皇の御前で火鉢に炭火を入れる時は、火箸を使わず、直接
手で入れるのが作法である。しかし、浄衣（じょうえ、神前で着る
白い狩衣の礼服）を着ている日は、火箸を使ってよいと有職故
実に詳しい人が言った」という段。火や箸の扱い方には、多くの
禁忌があった。

Essay 213.

Sumibi toru

    te to kariginu no

        ito shiroshi

Picking up the charcoal

    the hand and the silk kimono

        are purely white

Season word: sumibi (charcoal; all winter)

Kenkō-hōshi says, "A court attendant should not use metal chopsticks to place charcoal in the presence of an emperor, but he should pick it up by hand. As an exception, it is alright for the attendant to use metal chopsticks when he wears white silk attire."

第二百十四段

華清宮

　　楊貴妃の見し

　　　古代蓮

かせいきゅう

　　ようきひしのみし

　　　こだいはす

季語　古代蓮（こだいはす、遺跡で発見された実が開花
した蓮の総称、晩夏）

「想夫恋」という雅楽は、元は、「相府蓮」（相府は、中国・唐で「大
臣」のこと）であると考証する段。中国の王倹（452 年－489 年）とい
う学者・大臣が失脚した時、自分が清廉であることを泥の中に咲く
蓮に喩えたことに因んで、「相府蓮」という曲が作られた。これが、
転じて、「想夫恋」となった。この句は、唐（都は長安、現、西安）の
玄宗帝が楊貴妃（719 年－756 年）のために造った離宮を詠む。

Essay 214.

Kasei kyū

   Yō kihi no mishi

      kodai hasu

Huaqing Palace

   the ancient lotus blossoms

      that Yang Guifei had admired

Season word: kodai hasu (lotus grown from seeds found in
ancient ruins; late summer)
Kenkō-hōshi says that the word "ren" in the ancient music, *Sōfu-
ren*, originally meant lotus, not love. This originates in the story
based on the Chinese scholar/state minister Wang Jian (452–489),
who proclaimed his innocence when he was demoted, by
likening himself to the lotus that bloomed in the mud. This
haiku refers to the imperial villa Emperor Xuanzong of China's
Tang dynasty made for his consort Yang Guifei (719–756).

第二百十五段

最明寺

　　酒の肴は

　　　　味噌と花

さいみょうじ

　　さけのさかなは

　　　　みそとはな

季語　　花（はな、花は桜のこと、晩春）
鎌倉幕府第9代執権北条貞時の連署（れんしょ、執権の補佐役）、
大仏宣時（おさらぎのぶとき、北条宣時、歌人、1238年-1323年）
が、第5代執権北条時頼（貞時の祖父、1227年-1263年）に酒の
相手として呼ばれた時の段。酒の肴は何もなく、味噌を肴としたと
いう。時頼は、別荘を最明寺と改めて出家したため、最明寺入道と
呼ばれた。今日、「紫陽花寺」として知られる明月院は、最明寺の
塔頭（たっちゅう、本寺の境内にある小院）の一つであった。

Essay 215.

Saimyō ji

    sake no sakana wa

        miso to hana

Saimyō Temple

    the appetizers for sake are

        only miso and cherry blossoms

Season word: hana (*lit.*, "flower," refers to cherry blossoms; late spring)

This episode tells of the frugality of the Kamakura shogunate government officials. When Osaragi Nobutoki (1238–1323), the assistant to the ninth regent Hōjō Sadatoki, was invited by the retired fifth regent Hōjō Tokiyori (Sadatoki's grandfather, 1227–1263), the latter had no appetizer for sake so that they had sake with miso.

第二百十六段　1

いざ鎌倉

　　梅の鉢の木

　　　　急ぎたり

いざかまくら

　　うめのはちのき

　　　　いそぎたり

季語　　梅（うめ、初春）

鎌倉幕府第 5 代執権北条時頼（1227 年-1263 年）が、足利左馬
入道（義氏、1189 年-1255 年）の家に立ち寄った時の段。質素倹
約に励む鎌倉武士の厚い主従関係を示す。この句は、時頼の有
名な「鉢木」の逸話を詠む。時頼が僧となって諸国行脚した際、下
野佐野で貧しい武士、佐野源左衛門常世の家に泊まる。佐野は、
大切な梅、松、桜の鉢の木を燃やして暖をとらせたが、「鎌倉から
召集があれば、馳せ参ぜられるよう、武具と馬は残してある」と語っ
た。その後、時頼は、鉢の木に因んだ三つの所領を佐野に与えた。

Essay 216-1.

Iza Kamakura

   ume no hachi no ki

     isogi tari

Now to Kamakura

   The plum-tree-pot samurai

     was hurrying

Season word: ume (plum blossoms; early spring)

This essay tells the bond between Kamakura shogunate fifth regent Hōjō Tokiyori (1227–1263) and his retainer Ashikaga Yoshiuji (1189–1255). This haiku refers to a story "Potted Trees." When Tokiyori was travelling as a monk, he stayed overnight with a warrior, Sano Genzaemon Tsuneyo, who cut his precious bonsai trees and burned them as wood for the guest. He was poor but had kept worn-out armour and a horse in case the Kamakura shogunate called for a war. When the shogunate did call, Sano hurried to Kamakura and found that the monk was Tokiyori. Sano was given three pieces of land for cutting his three potted trees for Tokiyori.

第二百十六段　2

銀杏散る

　　八幡宮の

　　　　実朝と

いちょうちる

　　はちまんぐうの

　　　　さねともと

季語　　銀杏散る（いちょうちる、晩秋）

表向きは結束の固い鎌倉武士の主従関係が、実は脆弱であった
例として、前段の北条時頼の子孫、高時（第 14 代執権、1304 年-
1333 年）は、前段の足利義氏の子孫、尊氏（1305 年-1358 年）に
滅ぼされた。この句は、鎌倉幕府第 3 代将軍源実朝（1192 年-
1219 年）が、兄、第 2 代将軍頼家の子、公暁（1200 年-1219 年）
に暗殺されたことを詠む。鎌倉幕府初期の熾烈な権力抗争。

Essay 216-2.

Ichō chiru

    Hachiman gū no

        Sanetomo to

The gingko leaves fell

    at Hachiman Shrine

        with Sanetomo

Season word: ichō chiru (gingko leaves fall; late autumn)

The seeming solidarity of the Kamakura shogunate was fragile. Hōjō Takatoki (the 14th regent, 1304–1333), a descendent of Tokiyori, was defeated by Ashikaga Takauji (1305–1358), a descendent of Ashikaga Yoshiuji. This haiku refers to the power struggle of the Kamakura shogunate in which the third shogun Minamoto no Sanetomo (1192–1219) was assassinated by his nephew Kugyō (1200–1219) at Tsuruoka Hachiman Shrine.

第二百十七段

宝船

　　　　七福神の

　　　　　　夢枕

たからぶね

　　　しちふくじんの

　　　　　ゆめまくら

季語　宝船（たからぶね、新年）

ある大福長者が、「人は富を得ることを目指すべきである。しか
し、人間の欲望には際限が無いので、欲望を抑え、蓄えた富を
むやみに使ってはならない」と言ったことに対し、「欲望があって
も叶えず、財産があっても使わないのは、貧乏人と同じである。
だから、やはり財産は無い方がよい」と反論する兼行法師。

Essay 217.

Takara bune

   Shichi fukujin no

      yume makura

The treasure boat

   the Seven Gods of Fortune

      appear in the new year's dream

Season word: takara bune (treasure boat; new year)

A millionaire said, "Man should try to amass a fortune because this motivates him. But man's desires know no limit, so he should control his desires and should not use his fortune freely." Kenkō-hōshi opposes this by saying, "If he does not spend his fortune and does not fulfill his desires, he is the same as a poor man. It is better not to have a fortune, to begin with."

Chapter 8

Photograph 8: "Shira-bōshi" (Court Dancer Lady Shizuka), c. 1825, Katsushika Hokusai (c. 1760–1849), licensed by Wikimedia Commons, https://ja.wikipedia.org/wiki/静御前 #/media/ファイル:Shizuka-gozen_in_her_farewell_ dance_ to_Yoshitsune.jpg.

第二百十八段

狐火や

　　　賢治の森の

　　　　　幻燈会

きつねびや

　　　けんじのもりの

　　　　　げんとうかい

季語　狐火（きつねび、三冬）

狐が人に喰いついたという逸話。狐は非常に用心深い動
物で通常は人に襲いかかることはない。この句は、宮澤賢
治（1896 年-1933 年）の童話、『雪渡り』（1921 年 12 月初
出）を引用。子供と子狐の暖かい交流を描く珠玉の名作。

Essay 218.

Kitsune bi ya

Kenji no mori no

gentō kai

The foxfire

the magic lantern show

in the forest of Kenji

Season word: kitsune bi (foxfire; all winter)

Kenkō-hōshi tells of an episode in which a fox allegedly attacked
a man. In reality, foxes are very cautious and do not attack
humans. This haiku refers to the story *Yuki watari* (Snow
Crossing) by Miyazawa Kenji (1896–1933), in which children
are invited to a magic lantern show of a fox kit school in the
forest and found that foxes are gentle and honest creatures.

第二百十九段

鶯や

　　　笛吹童子

　　　　渡る橋

うぐいすや

　　　ふえふきどうじ

　　　　わたるはし

季語　　鶯（うぐいす、三春）

雅楽に用いる横笛の吹き方について、笛や笙（しょう、雅楽に使
う管楽器）の専門家の意見を披露する段。この句は、北村寿夫
（ひさお、1895 年-1982 年）の小説、『笛吹童子』（1953 年）を詠
む。主人公は、師匠から授かった春鶯囀（しゅんおうてん）という
名笛を吹き、応仁の乱（1467 年-1477 年）で荒廃した都の
人々の心を洗ったという。

Essay 219.

Uguisu ya

    fuefuki dōji

        wataru hashi

The bush warbler

    the flute player is crossing

        the bridge in Kyoto

Season word: uguisu (Japanese bush warbler; all spring)

Kenkō-hōshi expounds how to play the ancient flute. This haiku
refers to the novel *Fuefuki dōji* (Flute Player) by Kitamura Hisao
(1895–1982), in which the protagonist played the famed flute
given to him by his master and consoled people in Kyoto during
the long Battle of Ōnin (1467–1477).

第二百二十段

涅槃会や

　　　　四天王寺の

　　　　　　　　鐘祈る

ねはんえや

　　　　してんのうじの

　　　　　　　　かねいのる

季語　　涅槃会、ねはんえ、釈迦入滅の日の法会、旧暦、
二月十五日、仲春）
楽人の秘伝を紹介し、鐘の音は、黄鐘調（おうしきじょう、雅楽の音
階の一つ）でなければならないと説く段。「黄鐘調は、四天王寺（聖
徳太子創建）の六時堂のように、涅槃会（二月十五日）と精霊会
（聖徳太子の忌日の法会（二月二十二日）の間の中間音を基準と
して音階を調える」という。

Essay 220.

Nehan e ya

   Shiten'nō ji no

      kane inoru

The memorial day of Buddha's death

   the bell for the prayer

      at Shiten'nō Temple

Season word: Nehan e (memorial day of Buddha's death, February 15 in the old calendar, which corresponds to around March 15 today; mid-spring)

Quoting a court musician, Kenkō-hōshi says, "The sound of a temple bell should adhere to the ancient scale, *ōshiki-jō*, which is tuned to the median sound between the memorial day of Buddha's death (February 15) and that of Prince Shōtoku (574–622, February 22), as with the bell at Shiten'nō Temple founded by the latter.

154

第二百二十一段

蜘蛛の糸

　　罪人放つ

　　　　検非違使庁

くものいと

　　ざいひんじはなつ

　　　　けびいしちょう

季語　蜘蛛の糸（くものいと、蜘蛛の巣、三夏）

「賀茂祭の警護に当たらせた放免（元罪人で、検非違使庁の下僕）が、馬を象った風変わりな飾りを付け、蜘蛛の巣を描いた水干（丈の短い狩衣）を着て、この装束にまつわる短歌を吟じながら練り歩いたのを良く観たが、とても面白かった」という年老いた下級士官の思い出話の段。この句は、芥川龍之介（1892 年–1927 年）の小説、『蜘蛛の糸』を引く。

Essay 221.

Kumo no ito

    zainin hanatsu

        Kebiishi chō

The spider's thread

    the Police and Prosecutor's Agency

        has released the criminals

Season word: kumo no ito (spider's thread; all summer)

Kenkō-hōshi tells what a senior officer told him: "The Police and Prosecutor's Agency had former criminals serve as guards for the Kamo Festival. They wore fancy kimonos, with a design of spider's webs, carried ornaments in the shape of horses, and recited a poem related to their costume, as they marched. It was amusing." This haiku alludes to the story *Kumo no ito* (The Spider's Thread) by Akutagawa Ryūnosuke (1892–1927).

第二百二十二段

菩提樹や

　　　陀羅尼唱へる

　　　　　　中宮さま

ぼだいじゅや

　　　だらにとなえる

　　　　　　ちゅうぐうさま

季語　　菩提樹（ぼだいじゅ、仲夏）

竹谷乗願房（宗源、1168 年-1251 年）は、真言宗から改宗し浄土
宗の開祖法然に帰依したが、東二条院公子（後深草天皇の中宮、
1232 年-1304 年）から、「追善供養には何をするのが御利益があ
るか」と問われ、法然の唱えた単純な専修念仏ではなく、勿体振っ
て、難解な真言密教の「光明真言（こうみょうしんごん）と宝篋院陀
羅尼（ほうきょういんだらに）を唱えることであると答えた」という段。
この句の菩提樹の花は、淡黄色で芳香があり、実は数珠となる。

Essay 222.

Bodaiju ya

   Darani tonaeru

      Chūgū sama

The bodhi tree

   Empress Kimiko

      is chanting the Dharani

Season word: bodai tree (bodhi tree, sacred fig; mid-summer)

This episode is about Monk Sōgen (1168–1251) who was converted from esoteric Shingon Buddhism to simpler Pure Land Buddhism propagated by Saint Hōnen. Yet, when Empress Kimiko (1232–1304) asked him, "What is the best to way to pray for the dead," he answered to chant the Dharani and other Shingon texts, instead of a simple prayer as prescribed by Saint Hōnen, out of pride.

第二百二十三段

鶴ヶ城

　　　白虎を偲ぶ

　　　　　鶴一羽

つるがじょう

　　　びゃっこをしのぶ

　　　　　つるいちわ

季語　　鶴（つる、三冬）
「鶴の大臣（たづのおおい）殿と呼ばれる内大臣九条基家
（1203 年-1280 年）は、幼名が鶴君であったからそう呼ばれるの
であり、鶴を飼っていたからでは無い」と説く段。この句は、戊辰
戦争の激戦地となった鶴ヶ城（現、福島県会津若松市）と飯盛
山で自刃した白虎隊の若き志願兵を詠む。

Essay 223.

Tsuru ga jō

    Byakko o shinobu

        tsuru ichiwa

Tsuruga Castle

    the White Tiger Troop

        the lone crane reminiscences about them

Season word: tsuru (crane, red-crowned crane; all winter)

Kenkō-hōshi explains that Minister of the Right Kujō Motoie (1203–1280) is called "Lord Crane Minister" after his childhood name Prince Crane, not because he raised cranes. This haiku refers to Tsuruga Castle ("Crane Castle") in Aizu–Wakamatsu (in current Fukushima prefecture) where low-teenaged volunteer soldiers, the White Tigers, lost their lives to the new Meiji government troops in the Boshin War of 1868–1869.

第二百二十四段

花秋葵

　　　法師耕す

　　　　　畑の奥

はなおくら

　　ほうしたがやす

　　　　はたのおく

季語　　花秋葵（はなおくら、トロロアオイ、初秋）
陰陽師（おんみょうじ）安倍晴明（921 年–1005 年）の子孫で、
陰陽寮頭安倍有宗入道が、鎌倉から上京して、兼好法師の家
を訪ねた際、庭が無駄に広いことに呆れ返り、「細道一つを残し
て、畑を作りなさい」と諫言されたことに同意したという段。この
句の花秋葵は、淡黄色の美しい花で、花野菜として食用にされ
る。根は漢方薬として利用される。

Essay 224.

Hana okura

    hōshi tagayasu

        hata no oku

The sunset hibiscus blooms

    at the back of the vegetable garden

        the monk is plowing

Season word: hana okura (sunset hibiscus, aibika; early autumn)

The Divination Department head Abe no Arimune, descendent of famed diviner Abe no Haruaki (921–1005), visited Kyoto from Kamakura. As he saw Kenkō-hōshi's house, he was appalled by his vast empty garden and advised that he plant vegetables in the garden.

第二百二十五段

白菊や

　　　隠岐に届かむ

　　　　　その香り

しらぎくや

　　　おきにとどかん

　　　　　そのかおり

季語　白菊（しらぎく、三秋）

白拍子の由来について考証する段。小納言藤原通憲入道
（1106 年–1160 年、信西、しんぜい）が、磯禅師（いそのぜんじ）
という女性に教えた男舞（白い水干に烏帽子をつけて舞う）をそ
の娘、静（後の静御前）が継いだのが起源という。この句は、隠
岐に流された後鳥羽院に随行した白拍子、亀菊を詠む。

Essay 225.

Shira giku ya

    Oki ni todokan s

        ono kaori

The white chrysanthemum

    Send its fragrance

        to Oki Island

Season word: shira giku (white chrysanthemum; all autumn)

This essay is about the origin of the female court dancer called "shira byōshi." Fujiwara no Michinori (Shinzei, 1106–1160) taught a male dance to the female Iso no Zenji, who taught it to her daughter Shizuka. This haiku refers to the court dancer Kamegiku, who accompanied Retired Emperor Toba on his exile to Oki Island.

第二百二十六段

沙羅の花

　　　盛者必衰の

　　　　　世を悼む

しゃらのはな

　　しょうじゃひっすいの

　　　よをいたむ

季語　　沙羅の花（しゃらのはな、晩夏）

源平の盛衰を描いた『平家物語』の作者を考証する段。「信濃前
司行長（ゆきなが）が、侮辱を受けて官職を辞し、天台座主慈鎮
（慈円、1155 年–1225 年）の庇護のもと執筆し、生仏（しょうぶつ）と
いう盲目の僧に教えて語らせたものである」と書く。これは、藤原行
長のことではないかと言われるが、行長は信濃守ではなく、下野守
であった。この句の沙羅の花は、仏教の聖樹、「沙羅双樹」（釈迦
の入滅した木）の代わりとして、日本の寺院に植えられる。

Essay 226.

Shara no hana

    shōja hissui no

        yo o itamu

The stewartia blossoms

    mourn the world

        in which the ruler never fails to fall

Season word: shara no hana (Japanese stewartia; late summer)

This essay studies the author of *Heike monogatari* (The Tale of the Heike). He writes that a former Shinano governor Yukinaga wrote it and had the blind monk Shōbutsu recite it with biwa accompaniment, but this is not established. The Japanese stewartia in this haiku is planted in Buddhist temples in Japan as a substitute for the sacred sal tree in India.

Chapter 9

Photograph 9: "Kitsune no yomeiri" (Fox Wedding), Katsushika Hokusai (c. 1760–1849), licensed by Wikimedia Commons,https://ja.wikipedia.org/wiki/狐の嫁入り#/media/ファイル:Hokusai_Kitsune-no-yomeiri.jpg.

第二百二十七段

赤啄木鳥か

　　偈頌の木霊か

　　　　鹿ヶ谷

あかげらか

　　げじゅのこだまか

　　　　ししがだに

季語　赤啄木鳥（あかげら、アカゲラ、三秋）
浄土宗の「一念の念仏」の起源を考証する段。法然の弟子安楽房
遵西（じゅんさい）と住蓮（じゅうれん）が、「六時礼讃」（一日を六つ
に分けて、阿弥陀仏礼讃の偈頌を唱える）を東山鹿谷で勤行とし
て始めた。その後、僧侶太秦善観房が、その偈頌に高低、抑揚、
節を付けて声明（しょうみょう）にした。これが「一念の念仏」由来。

Essay 227.

Aka gera ka

  geju no kodama ka

   Shishi ga dani

Is it the woodpecker's singing

  or the monk's chanting

   in Shishi valley

Season word: aka gera (great spotted woodpecker; all autumn)
This essay tells of the origin of the "prayer for one belief" of Pure Land Buddhism. Hōnen's disciples, Junsai and Jūren, began the practice "six-times a day prayer" in Shishi valley. Then Kanbō gave it a chant tone. This became the "prayer for one belief" chanting.

第二百二十八段

遺教会

　　　おかめの像の

　　　　　手を合わす

　　ゆいきょうえ

　　　おかめのぞうの

　　　　　てをあわす

季語　遺教会（ゆいきょうえ、遺教経会、仲春）
遺教経会（ゆいきょうぎょうえ、千本釈迦念仏）の起源についての
段。これは、京都の大報恩寺（千本釈迦堂）で 2 月 9 日から 15 日
まで行われた涅槃会（釈迦入滅日の法会）で、釈迦の最後の教え
である遺教経を講じ、大念仏を修した。浄土宗の如輪（にょりん）上
人（大報恩寺二代長老澄空）が始めた。現在は、3 月 22 日に行う。
この句は、大報恩寺の本堂を建てた棟梁を助け、命を絶った妻お
かめの逸話を詠む。

Essay 228.

Yuikyō e

    Okame no zō no

       te o awasu

The grand memorial service for Buddha's death

    the statue of Okame

       offers prayers

Season word: Yuikyō e (a grand memorial service for

Buddha's death, March 22; mid-spring)

This essay tells of the origin of the Yuikyō-gyō e, a grand

memorial service for Buddha's death, conducted from February

9–15 in the old calendar, at Daihō'on Temple in Kyoto. This

haiku refers to the statue of Okame, the wife of the carpenter

who built the temple. She sacrificed her life in helping him.

第二百二十九段

針槐

　　妙観の彫る

　　　　千手観音

はりえんじゅ

　　みょうかんのほる

　　　　せんじゅかんのん

季語　　針槐（はりえんじゅ、ニセアカシア、初夏）
妙観という名工のように、腕の良い細工人は、少し鈍い刀を使う
と言う段。比丘（修行僧）妙観は、780年、摂津国（現、大阪府
箕面市）にある勝尾寺（かつおうじ、弥勒寺）に、白檀香木から
十一面千手観音像を彫った。これが当寺の本尊となり、その香
木も現在、安置されている。この句の針槐は甘い芳香を放つ。

Essay 229.

Hari enju

 Myōkan no horu

  Senju kan'non

The black locust

 Myōkan is carving the statue

  of the One thousand-handed Goddess of Mercy

Season word: hari enju (black locust; early summer)

This essay tells that master sculptors such as Myōkan use dull
knives. Myōkan made a statue of the eleven-faced one
thousand-handed Goddess of Mercy, out of an aromatic tree, at
Katsuo Temple in Settsu (Minō, Osaka prefecture), which exists
today. Black locust in this haiku has a sweet aroma.

第二百三十段

狐雨

　　　　白き提灯

　　　　　　長き列

きつねあめ

　　　しろきちょうちん

　　　　　ながきれつ

季語　狐雨（きつねあめ、狐の嫁入り、天気雨、仲夏）
権大納言二条為世（ためよ、1250 年-1338 年、兼好法師の和歌の
師）によると、「亀山天皇（1249 年-1305 年）の五条里内裏で、狐が
人のように跪いて御簾を掲げて中を覗いていた。人が騒ぐと慌てて
逃げた」と言う段。この句の狐雨（別名、狐の嫁入り）は、天気雨が、
狐に化かされたような不思議な現象であることに由来。

Essay 230.

Kitsune ame

   shiroki chōchin

      nagaki retsu

The shower on the fine day

   the white lanterns

      and the long processions

Season word: kitsune ame (*lit*, "fox rain" refers to a
shower on a fine day; mid-summer)
Kenkō-hōshi's poetry teacher, Nijō Tameyo (1250–1338), told
that an impersonating fox appeared in the Imperial Palace of
Emperor Kameyama (1249–1305), raised the screen and peeped
inside, but ran away when people made a commotion. This
haiku is about the shower on a fine day, which was considered a
fox's mischief and a fox wedding procession, because it
mysteriously appears and disappears quickly.

第二百三十一段

寒の鯉

　　桐の柾目の

　　　　俎板へ

かんのこい

　　きりのまさめの

　　　　まないたへ

季語　　寒の鯉（かんのこい、かんごい、晩冬）
比類なき料理の名人、園（その）の別当入道、権大納言藤原基
氏（もとうじ、1211年–1282年）が、鯉の包丁捌きを披露する際、
周りの空気を読んだ口上に皆、感心したが、北山太政入道（西
園寺実兼、さねかね、1249年–1322年）は快く思わず、「勿体
振らずに、直截に言った方がよかった」と言ったことに納得する
兼好法師。この句は、寒中が最も美味とされる鯉を詠む。

Essay 231.

Kan no koi

    kiri no masame no

        manaita e

The winter carp

    was being placed

        on the cutting board made of paulownia

Season word: kan no koi (winter carp; late winter)

Fujiwara no Motouji (1211–1282), a master chef, made a
clever and considerate remark when he volunteered to
carve carp for cooking, and people were impressed. But
Saionji Sanekane (1249–1322, Chancellor in 1291)
commented that he should have said it simply. Kenkō-
hōshi concurs. Carp is considered most delicious in winter.

第二百三十二段

虞美人草

　　　弦を爪弾く

　　　　琵琶法師

ぐびじんそう

　　　げんをつまびく

　　　　びわほうし

季語　虞美人草（ぐびじんそう、ひなげし、三夏）
「人は、全て無智無能であるべきで、人前で賢そうに振る舞うことは見苦しい。ある琵琶奏者の知ったかぶりの態度は、傍目にも恥じ入ることであった」と言う兼好法師。この句は、古代中国漢の英雄劉邦に敗れ、四面楚歌となった楚の武将項羽の愛姫、虞姫の鮮血が化して虞美人草となったと言う伝説を引く。

Essay 232.

Gubijin sō

    gen o tsuma biku

        biwa hōshi

The red poppy

    the biwa player

        is plucking the string

Season word: gubijin sō ('yu mei ren' in Chinese after

Consort Yu, red poppy; all summer)

After observing a proud biwa player, Kenkō-hōshi wrote that a
man should know of his ignorance and that it was unpleasant to
see a man behaving like a "know it all." This haiku refers to an
ancient Chinese legend: As the warlord Xiang Yu was defeated
in 202 BC, his consort Yu committed suicide and her blood was
transformed into a red poppy.

第二百三十三段

落椿

　　　　寂光院の

　　　　　　　花手水

おちつばき

　　　　じゃっこういんの

　　　　　　　はなちょうず

季語　　落椿（おちつばき、三春）

「物事に非がないようにしたければ、何事にも誠意を持って接し、人を差別せず、敬い、言葉少なくするのが一番である」という兼好法師。この句は、京都市大原にある天台宗の尼寺、寂光院を詠む。平清盛の娘、建礼門院徳子（1155 年–1214 年）が、平家滅亡後、隠棲し、一門の菩提を弔った寺。椿は、花びらが散るのではなく、花が丸ごと落ちるので、落椿と呼ばれる。

Essay 233.

Ochi tsubaki

    Jakkō in no

        hana te mizu

The fallen camellia

    on the handwashing basin

        at Jakkō Temple

Season word: ochi tsubaki (fallen camellia; all spring)

Kenkō-hōshi says that if one wants to avoid criticism, he should treat people with sincerity and respect and should not be talkative. This haiku refers to the daughter of Taira no Kiyomori (1118–1181), Kenreimon-in Tokushi (1155–1214), who prayed for the souls of her son Emperor Antoku (1178–1185) and other family members at Jakkō Temple in Kyoto.

第二百三十四段

香嵐渓

　　首を傾げる

　　　　堅香子の花

こうらんけい

　　くびをかたげる

　　　　かたかごのはな

季語　　堅香子の花（かたかご、片栗の古名、初春）

「人に何か聞かれたら、自分にとっては簡単なことでも、それを
知らない人はいるので、わかりやすく明快に答えてあげるのがよ
い」と説く兼好法師。この句は、カタクリ群生地のある愛知県豊
田市足助町（あすけちょう）の香嵐渓（紅葉の名所）を詠む。

Essay 234.

Kōran kei

    kubi o katageru

        katakago no hana

Kōran valley

    the Asian fawnlily

        is tilting its neck

Season word: katakago no hana (Asian fawnlily, dogtooth violet; early spring)

Kenkō-hōshi says, "When you are asked a question, you had better answer it in earnest because people might not know things you take it for granted." This haiku refers to the valley, Kōrankei, in Asuke-chō, Toyota, Aichi prefecture, known for its colony of Asian fawnlily and fall foliage.

第二百三十五段

水澄し

　　明鏡止水の

　　　　湖の宿

みずすまし

　　めいきょうしすいの

　　　　うみのやど

季語　水澄し（みずすまし、あめんぼう、三夏）
「鏡にはそれ自体の色や形が無いので、あらゆる物の姿が映る。空気は空っぽなので、何でも物が入いる。同様に、空っぽな人の心には邪念が入いる。自分の心持ちがしっかりしていれば、雑念が入る隙はない」と説く兼好法師。この句の「明鏡止水」は、邪念のない心境を表す言葉。

Essay 235.

Mizu sumashi

    meikyō shisui no

        umi no yado

The water strider

    lives on the lake

        with the clear water like a mirror

Season word: mizu sumashi (water strider; all summer)

Kenkō-hōshi writes that if your mind is firm, there is no room for worldly thoughts to get into your mind. This haiku quotes the words of a politician, "My mind is as clear as water like a mirror," when he was implicated in a financial scandal.

Chapter 10

Photograph 10: "Painting of White Plum Blossoms and Red Camelias for Essay 237, *Tsurezure-gusa*," 1800–1850, Art Institute of Chicago, licensed by Picryl, https://picryl. com/media/passage-237-nihyaku-sanjunana-dan-from-the-series-essays-in-idleness-for-the-203801.

第二百三十六段

初詣

　　獅子と狛犬

　　　　神妙に

はつもうで

　　ししとこまいぬ

　　　　しんみょうに

季語　　初詣（はつもうで、新年）
丹波の出雲神社（現、京都府亀山市、出雲大社を勧請したもの）
に詣でた聖海（しょうかい）上人の逸話の段。社の獅子（左側）と
狛犬（右側）の位置が通常と異なり、後ろ向きに座っていたのを
見て、何か特別な深い謂れがあるのだろうと思い、感涙した。社
の年配の神官に理由を聞くと、「単なる子供の悪戯である」と言
い、さっさと位置を据え直して去って行ったという話。

Essay 236.

Hatsu mōde

   shishi to komainu

     shinmyō ni

New Year's Day

   the lion and the lion-dog

     sit solemnly

Season word: hatsu mōde (a visit to a shrine on New Year's Day; new year)

This is an episode about Saint Shōkai, who went to Izumo Shrine in Kyoto (a branch shrine of Izumo Grand Shrine) and found the stone statues of the lion and the lion-dog sitting facing backwards (as opposed to facing to the front). Thinking that this must have a special history, he was touched and shed tears. He asked about this to a senior priest there, who flatly said, "This was a child's mischief." He corrected the position of the two statues and left.

第二百三十七段

書初めや

　　縦横に置く

　　　　筆硯

かきぞめや

　　たてよこにおく

　　　　ふですずり

季語　書初め（かきぞめ、新年）

柳筥（やないばこ、柳の枝を並べて生糸で結んで仕立てた蓋付の
箱）の蓋の上に物を置く作法について、縦様（柳の枝と並行に置く）
か、横様（直角に置く）かについて考証する段。「三条右大臣は縦
に置くと言ったが、勘解由小路家（かでのこうじけ、能書家、藤原行
成の子孫）は、全て横に置いた」という。

191

Essay 237.

Kaki zome ya

    tate yoko ni oku

        fude suzuri

First calligraphy of the year

    placing the inkbrush and the inkstone

        crosswise and lengthwise

Season word: kaki zome (first calligraphy of the year; new year)

Kenkō-hōshi examines the decorum of how to place items on the cover of the willow box. Minister of the Right Sanjō put them lengthwise, whereas the Kade-no-kōji family, the descendants of the famed calligrapher Fujiwara no Yukinari (972–1028), put everything crosswise, never lengthwise.

第二百三十八段

白木槿

　　　袂を分ち

　　　　　袖にする

しろむくげ

　　　たもとをわかち

　　　　　そでにする

季語　木槿（むくげ、初秋）

兼好法師が7つの自慢話を披露する段。その中に、「袖と袂と言う
同じ意味の言葉を一首に詠んでもよいか」という後鳥羽院の問い
に対して、藤原定家（1162年-1241年）は、袖と袂を含む歌を引用
し、「全く問題ない」と答えたという逸話がある。この句は、茶道の始
祖、千利休の孫千宗旦（そうたん、1578年-1658年）の子が、三千
家（武者小路千家、表千家、裏千家）に分派したことを引く。侘（わ
び）の極限を説いた宗旦は、白い木槿、「宗旦木槿」を愛でた。

Essay 238.

Sōtan mukuge

  tamoto o wakachi

    sode ni suru

The Sōtan rose of Sharon

  splits the sleeves

    and abandons them

Season word: mukuge (rose of Sharon, *hibiscus syriacus*;
early autumn)

This essay includes an episode of Retired Emperor Go-Toba (1180–
1391). He asked Fujiwara no Teika (1162–1241) whether it was
alright to use two words that had same meaning ('sode' and
'tamoto' both mean sleeves). Quoting a poem that used the two
words, Teika said, "No problem." This haiku refers to the tea
ceremony master Sen no Sōtan (1578–1658), the grandson of Sen
no Rikyū. Sōtan's sons split and created their own schools. Sōtan
loved the simplicity of white rose of Sharon or Sōtan mukuge.

第二百三十九段

栗名月

　　　伊那の里山

　　　　栗の山

くりめいげつ

　　　いなのさとやま

　　　　くりのやま

季語　栗名月（くりめいげつ、旧暦九月十三夜の月、晩秋）　栗の山（くりのやま、晩秋）
「八月十五日と九月十三日は、婁宿（ろうしゅく、古代中国の天文学で黄道に沿った二十八の星座――二十八宿――の一つ。西方七宿の二番目の宿。牡羊座。和名、たたら星）という清く明るい宿にあたるので、月を愛でるのにふさわしい夜である」と説く兼行法師。この句の「栗名月」は、中秋の名月（八月十五夜の月）の対として愛でられてきた。岐阜県伊那市は、栗の名産地。

Essay 239.

Kuri meigetsu

    Ina no satoyama

        kuri no yama

The Chestnut Moon

    the mountain village of Ina

        and the mountain of chestnuts

Season words: Kuri meigetsu (Chestnut Moon, moon on September 13 in the old calendar; late autumn) and kuri no yama (mountain of chestnuts; late autumn)
Kenkō-hōshi says that August 15 and September 13 belong to a clear and bright constellation per ancient Chinese astrology and that this accounts for the fine moons on these dates that are worth admiring. This haiku refers to Ina, Gifu prefecture, which is famous for chestnuts.

第二百四十段

朧月

　　蘭奢漂ふ

　　　　有明の空

おぼろづき

　　らんじゃただよう

　　　　ありあけのそら

季語　朧月（おぼろづき、三春）

「人目を忍んでの逢瀬には趣深いものがあるが、通い婚は煩わしく、見合い婚は味気なく不愉快である。花鳥風月を理解しない人は恋愛をしない方が良い」と手厳しく男女関係を講ずる兼好法師。この句の「蘭麝」は、蘭草（藤袴、フジバカマ）の乾燥葉と麝香（じゃこう）を混ぜた香料のこと。句中の「有明」は有明月のことではなく、単に夜明けを意味する。

Essay 240.

Oboro zuki

    ranja tadayo'u

        ariake no sora

The hazy moon

    the scent of ranja drifts

        into the lightening sky

Season word: oboro zuki (a hazy moon; all spring)

Kenkō-hōshi says, "A secret love affair is interesting, but marriage is unpleasant. A man who does not understand the aesthetic beauty of nature, he had better not get involved in love." This haiku refers to a perfume called 'ranja,' a mix of dried leaves of fragrant eupatorium and musk.

第二百四十一段

本能寺

　　明智の里の

　　　　桔梗泣く

ほんのうじ

　　あけちのさとの

　　　　ききょうなく

季語　桔梗（ききょう、「秋の七草」の一つ、初秋）
「満月がすぐ欠けてしまうように死は目前にあるにも拘らず、人
は限りない願いを成就しようとして迷いの道から抜け出せないで
いる。この邪念を捨てて仏の道に入れば、心身の安寧が得られ
る」と説く兼好法師。この句は、本能寺の変（1582 年）で暴君と
化した織田信長を討つも、その 11 日後に斬られた明智光秀
（1528 年–1582 年）の悲哀を詠む。明智家の家紋は水色桔梗。

Essay 241.

Hon'nō ji

   Akechi no sato no

      kikyō naku

Hon'nō Temple

   the balloon flower

      in the field of Akechi cries

Season word: kikyō (balloon flower; early autumn)

Kenkō-hōshi says, "As a full moon soon wanes, a man's death is fast approaching. Without realizing this, the man struggles to achieve limitless wishes. Once he abandons them and enters the world of Buddhism, he will attain peace of mind." This haiku refers to Akechi Mitsuhide (1528–1582), who assassinated his master, a tyrant-like Oda Nobunaga, at Hon'nō Temple, but soon was killed by a retainer of Nobunaga. Akechi's family crest was a blue balloon flower.

第二百四十二段

安土城

　　天主の夢と

　　　　散る桜

あずちじょう

　　てんしゅのゆめと

　　　　ちるさくら

季語　　散る桜（ちるさくら、晩春）

「三つの欲望（名声欲、性欲、食欲）を求めなければ、人は煩いや
苦しみから解放される」と諭す兼好法師。この句は、尾張国の武将
織田信長（1534 年-1582 年）が、1576 年、琵琶湖東岸に築いた安
土城（現、滋賀県近江八幡市）を詠む。威容を誇る絢爛華麗な城
であったが、本能寺の変（1582 年）後、焼失し、廃城となった。

Essay 242.

Azuchi jō

   tenshu no yume to

      chiru sakura

Azuchi Castle

   the dream of the castle tower

      and the falling cherry blossoms

Season word: chiru sakura (falling cherry blossoms; late spring)

Kenkō-hōshi says, "If a man does not seek the three desires (appetite, lust, and desire for fame), he will be liberated from his suffering." This haiku refers to the majestic Azuchi Castle that Nobunaga (1534–1582) built. After his assassination it was burned down and was abolished.

第二百四十三段

大賀蓮

　　　御仏の座す

　　　　　土と宇宙

おおがはす

　　　みほとけのざす

　　　　　つちとそら

季語　　大賀蓮（おおがはす、古代蓮の一種、晩夏）
兼好法師が８歳の時、父に仏の起源について問い続けて困らせたと言う段。兼好法師の父、卜部兼顕は、神祇官として後宇多天皇（1267 年-1324 年、在位 1274 年-1287 年）などに仕えた。この句の大賀蓮は、縄文時代の遺跡で発見された蓮の実を開花させた植物学者、大賀一郎（1883 年-1965 年）に因む。

Essay 243.

Ōga hatsu

    mi hotoke no zasu

        tsuchi to sora

The Ōga lotus blossoms

    the earth and the sky

        where Buddha resides

Season word: Ōga hatsu (a species of ancient lotus; late summer)

This last essay is the only personal one Kenkō-hōshi wrote. When he was eight years old, he kept asking about the origin of Buddha to his father, Urabe Kaneaki, who served as a priest for Emperor Go-Uda (1267–1324) and other emperors. This haiku refers to the ancient lotus seeds found in the ruins; the botanist Ōga Ichirō (1883–1965) succeeded in making them bloom.

Selected Bibliography

Sources in English

Carter, Steven D. Ed. and trans. *The Columbia Anthology of Japanese Essays: Zuihitsu from the Tenth to the Twenty-first Century*. New York, NY: Columbia University Press, 2014.

Chance, Linda H. *Formless in Form: Kenko, Tsurezuregusa, and the Rhetoric of Japanese Fragmentary Proses*. Stanford, CA: Stanford University Press, 1997.

Kenkō (Yoshida, Kenkō) and Chōmei (Kamo no Chōmei). *Essays in Idleness and Hōjōki*. Trans. by Meredith McKinney, New York, NY: Penguin Classics, 2014.

Sansom, George Bailey. *The Tsurezure Gusa of Yoshida No Kaneyoshi, Being the Meditations of a Recluse in the 14th Century*. London, UK: Asiatic Society of Japan, 1911.

Sato, Hiroaki. *Legends of the Samurai*. New York, NY: Harry N. Abrams, 2012.

Shirane, Haruo. Ed. *Traditional Japanese Literature: An Anthology, Beginnings to 1600.* New York, NY: Columbia University Press, 2007.

Yoshida Kenkō. *Essays in Idleness: The Tsurezuregusa of Kenkō.* Trans. by Donald Keene, New York, NY: Columbia University Press, 1967, 1998; North Clarendon, VT: Tuttle Classics, 2006.

Sources in Japanese

Gomi, Fumihiko. *Zōho Tsurezure-gusa no reishi gaku* (Study of the History of *Tsurezure-gusa,* Additional Printing). Tokyo: Kadokawa sofia-bunko, 2014.

Kaihō, Yūsetsu. Illustrations. Shimauchi Yūko. ed. Ekami de miru・yomu Tsurezure-gusa (To Watch and Read Tsurezure-gusa through Picture Scrolls). Translated and annotated by Ueno Tomoe, Tokyo: Asahi Shimbun-shuppan, 2016.

Keene, Donald. "'Tsurezure-gusa' ni miru bi ishiki" (The Aesthetics Seen in "Tsurezure-gusa"). *Tokyo Shimbun,* September 17, 2017.

Keene, Seiki (Echigo, Kakutayū). "Hibi Donarudo Kiin to tomonu" (Every Day with Donald Keene). "Karuizawa 17," September 4, 2017, https://echigo-kakutayu2.blog.ss-blog.jp/2017-09-23-2.

Nakano, Kōji. *Surasura yomeru Tsurezure-gusa* (Idle Essays: An Easy Reading. Tokyo: Kōdansha-bunko, 2013.

Sadaijin. "Tsurezure-gusa: Gendaigo yaku tsuki rōdoku (Idle Essays: Recitation with Modern Translations). June 5, 2015, https://roudokus.com/tsurezure/.

Shimauchi, Yūko. "Tsurezure-gusa byōbu no kenkyū: 'Atsuta byōbu' to 'Uesugi byōbu' o chūshin ni" (A Study of Folding-Panel Pictures for Tsurezure-gusa: "The Atsuta Folding-Panel Pictures" and "The Uesugi Folding-Panel Pictures"). Hōsō daigaku kenkyū nenpō, March 31, 2006, 23-010.pdf.

Sumioka, Teruaki. "'Tsurezure-gusa' no shippitsu haikei" (Background of "Tsurezure-gusa"). September 9, 2021, https://www.insightnow.jp/article/11299.

Terada, Torahiko. "Tsurezure-gusa no kanshō" (Analyses of Idle Essays). *Bungaku* (Literature), 1934; *Terada Torahiko zenshū*, Vol. 7, Tokyo: Iwanami-shoten, 1997; Tokyo: Aozora-bunko, 2012.

"Tsurezure-gusa DB" (Tsurezure-gusa Database). https://www2.yamanashi-ken.ac.jp/~itoyo/tsuredure/ turedure_index.htm, December 3, 2021.

"Tsurezure-gusa gendaigo yaku (kōgo yaku) to kaisetsu: Kenkō no yūmoa to kyōkun" (Modern Translations [Colloquial Japanese] and Analyses of Idle Essays: The Humor and Aphorisms of Kenkō). December 5, 2015– April 8, 2019, http://bookloid.com/essays-in-idleness/.

"Tsurezure-gusa no genbun naiyō to gendaigo yaku: Kenkō-hōshi no shōgai" (Content of the Original Text and Modern Translations of Idle Essays: Life of Kenkō-hōshi). "Shiki no bi" (Beauty of Four Seasons), April 27, 2021, https://shikinobi.com/kenkou.

"Tsurezure-gusa: Tsurezure naru mamani: Genbun · gendaigo yaku (Idle Essays: Just as Idle, with the Original Text and Modern Translations). December 3, 2020, http://

keirinkan-online.jp/high-classic-japanese/20201028/523/.

Ueno, Tomoe, Sasaki, Yasuyuki, and Uchida, Takeshi. eds.
Tsurezure-gusa: Bijutsu de tanoshimu koten bungaku
(Tsurezure-gusa: Japanese Classic Literature through The
Arts). Tokyo: Suntory Museum of Art, 2014.

Utsumi, Kōzō. *Tsurezure gusa shōkai* (Detailed Analyses
of Idle Essays). Tokyo: Meiji-shoin, 1948.
Yoshida Kenkō. Kadokawa-shoten, ed. *Tsurezure-gusa*
(Idle Essays). Tokyo: Kadokawa-shoten, 2002.

Yoshida, Kenkō. *Kaitei Tsurezure-gusa*: *Gendai goyaku
tsuki* (Idle Essays with Modern Translations, Revised
Edition). Translated and annotated by Imaizumi Tadayoshi,
Tokyo: Kadokawa-shoten, 1957, 1995.

Yoshida, Kenkō. *Tsurezure-gusa* (Idle Essays). Edited and
translated by Ichiko Teiji and Miki Sumito, Tokyo: Meiji-
shoin, 1970.

Yoshida, Kenkō. *Shinban Tsurezure-gusa*: *Gendai goyaku
tsuki* (Idle Essays with Modern Translations, New Edition).

Translated and annotated by Ogawa Takeo, Tokyo: Kadokawa sofia-bunko, 2015.

Yoshida, Kenkō. *Shintei Tsurezure-gusa* (Idle Essays, New Edition). Annotated by Nishio Minoru and Yasuraoka Kōsaku, Tokyo: Iwanami-bunko, 1985.

Yoshida, Kenkō. *Tsurezure-gusa* (Idle Essays). Translated by Azuma Toshiaki. May 21, 2016–April 5, 2018, https://www. tsurezuregusa.com.

Yoshida, Kenkō. *Tsurezure-gusa* (Idle Essays). Edited and translated by Shimauchi Yūko, Tokyo: Chikuma-shobō, 2010.

Yoshida, Kenkō and Kamo no Chōmei. *Hōjō-ki, Tsurezure-gusa* (Idle Essays and Hōjō-ki). Edited and translated by Miki Sumito, Tokyo: Shōgaku-tosho, 1980.

About the Author

Mayumi Itoh is a former Professor of Political Science at the University of Nevada, Las Vegas. She has preciously taught at Princeton University and Queens College, City University of New York. Her book titles include: *Globalization of Japan: Japanese Sakoku Mentality and U.S. Efforts to Open Japan* (1998); *The Hatoyama Dynasty: Japanese Political Leadership Through the Generations* (2003); *Japanese War Orphans in Manchuria: Forgotten Victims of World War II* (2010); *Japanese Wartime Zoo Policy: The Silent Victims of World War II* (2010); *The Origin of Ping-Pong Diplomacy* (2011); *Pioneers of Sino-Japanese Relations: Liao and Takasaki* (2012); *The Origins of Contemporary Sino-Japanese Relations: Zhou Enlai and Japan* (2016); *The Making of China's War with Japan: Zhou Enlai and Zhang Xueliang* (2016); *The Making of China's Peace with Japan* (2017); *Hachiko* (2017); *Kaneko Misuzu: Life and Poems of A Lonely Princess* (2018); *The Japanese Culture of Mourning Whales* (2018); *Animals and the Fukushima Nuclear Disaster* (2018); *Haikus of All Seasons*, Vol. I–Vol. XII (2018–2019); *Poems of Kaneko Misuzu and Haikus Inspired by Them*, Vol. I–Vol. IV (2019); *Haikus for Hiroshige's One Hundred Famous Scenes of Edo* (2020); *Spring and Asura* (2021); *Song of Circling The Stars* (2021); *The Narrow Road to The Deep North* (2021); *Essays in a Wood Backpack* (2021); *Journal of Weathered Bones in the Wilderness* (2021); and *Journal of Kashima and Journal of Sarashina* (2021).